REPORT OF THE
COMMISSION ON COUNTRY LIFE

REPORT OF THE
COMMISSION ON
COUNTRY LIFE

With an Introduction by

THEODORE ROOSEVELT

CHAPEL HILL

THE UNIVERSITY

OF NORTH CAROLINA

PRESS

Published March, 1911, by Sturgis & Walton
Reprinted September 1911, March 1917

Reprinted May, 1944

EXPLANATION

The Report of the Commission on Country Life was published as Senate Document No. 705, 60th Congress, 2d Session, for the use of Congress. It has not been available for popular distribution. The Spokane Chamber of Commerce has reprinted it, for use in the country life movement in the Northwest.

The Report is now placed in the hands of a regular book publisher, as one means of making an accessible record of the findings and recommendations of the Commission. If profits accrue to the Commission from the sale of the book, they will be devoted to public country life work.

L. H. BAILEY,
For the Commission.

ITHACA, N. Y., September 20, 1910.

INTRODUCTION

INTRODUCTION

SAGAMORE HILL,
OYSTER BAY, N. Y.
July 21st., 1910.

I am glad that the report of the Commission on Country Life is to be reprinted. I had hoped that Congress would make an appropriation to give the Commission official status and furnish it the means to continue its admirable work. As this was not done, I trust that so far as possible the work will be continued by private and voluntary aid. The Commissioners have served without compensation and they are entitled to the heartiest thanks from all men intelligently interested in the welfare of their country.

The Commission was appointed because the time has come when it is vital to the welfare of the country seriously to consider the problems of farm life. So far the farmer has not received the attention that the city worker has received and has not been able to express himself as the city worker has done. The problems of farm life have received very little consideration and the result has been bad for those who dwell in the open country, and therefore bad for the whole nation. We were founded as a nation of farmers, and in spite of the great growth of our industrial life it still remains true that our whole system rests upon the farm, that the welfare of the whole community depends upon the welfare of the farmer. The strengthening of country life is the strengthening of the whole nation.

If country life is to become all that it should be, if the career of a farmer is to rank with any other career in the country as a dignified and desirable way of earning a living, the farmer must take advantage of all that agricultural knowledge has to offer, and also of all that has raised the standard of living and of intelligence in other callings. We who are interested in this movement desire to take counsel with the farmer, as his fellow citizens, so as to see whether the nation cannot aid in this matter; for the city dweller in the long run has only less concern than the country dweller in how the country dweller fares. I am well aware that the working farmers themselves will in the last resort have to solve this problem for themselves; but as it also affects in only less degree all the rest of us, it is not merely our duty, but in our interest, to see if we can render any help towards making the solution satisfactory.

THEODORE ROOSEVELT.

INTRODUCTORY SUMMARY
OF THE REPORT

REPORT OF THE
COMMISSION ON COUNTRY LIFE

(Introductory Summary of Report, pages 17 to 31.)[1]

(The full Report of the Commission, pages 33 to 150.)

WASHINGTON, January 23, 1909.

To the President:

The Commission on Country Life herewith presents its report, covering the following topics:

INTRODUCTORY REVIEW OR SUMMARY. [Pages 17 to 31.]

FULL REPORT OF THE COMMISSION. [Pages 33 to 150.]

I. GENERAL STATEMENT.
 The purpose of the Commission. [Page 40.]
 Methods pursued by the Commission. [Page 49.]
 (Circulars, Hearings, School-house meetings.)

[1 The Introductory Summary or Review, with the President's Message, went to the press, and it is from this brief synopsis that the popular knowledge of the Commission's conclusions is derived.]

INTRODUCTORY REVIEW
OR SUMMARY

The Commission finds that agriculture in the United States, taken altogether, is prosperous commercially, when measured by the conditions that have obtained in previous years, although there are some regions in which this is only partially true. The country people are producing vast quantities of supplies for food, shelter, clothing, and for use in the arts. The country homes are improving in comfort, attractiveness and healthfulness. Not only in the material wealth that they produce, but in the supply of independent and strong citizenship, the agricultural people constitute the very foundation of our national efficiency. As agriculture is the immediate basis of country life, so it follows that the general affairs of the open country, speaking broadly, are in a condition of improvement.

Many institutions, organizations, and movements are actively contributing to the increasing welfare of the open country. The most important of these are the United States Department of Agriculture, the colleges of agriculture and the experiment stations in the states, and the national farmers' organizations. These institutions and organizations are now properly assuming leadership in country life affairs, and consequently in many of the public questions of national bearing. With these agencies must be mentioned state departments of agriculture, agricultural societies and organizations of very many kinds, teachers in schools, workers in church and other religious associations, travelling libraries, and many other groups, all working with commendable zeal to further the welfare of the people of the open country.

The Most Prominent Deficiencies.

Yet it is true, notwithstanding all this progress as measured by historical standards, that agriculture is not commercially as profitable as it is entitled to be for the labor and energy that the farmer expends and the risks that he assumes, and that the social conditions in the open country are far short of their possibilities. We must measure our agricultural efficiency by its possibilities rather than by comparison with previous conditions. The farmer is almost necessarily handicapped in the development of his business because his capital is small, and the volume of his transactions limited; and he usually stands practically alone against organized interests. In the general readjustment of modern life due to the great changes in manufactures and commerce, inequalities and discriminations have arisen, and naturally the separate man suffers most. The unattached man has problems that government should understand.

The reasons for the lack of a highly organized rural society are very many, as the full Report explains. The leading specific causes are:

A lack of knowledge on the part of farmers of the exact agricultural conditions and possibilities of their regions;

Lack of good training for country life in the schools;

The disadvantage or handicap of the farmer as against the established business systems and interests, preventing him from securing adequate returns for his products, depriving him of the benefits that would result from unmonopolized rivers and the conservation of forests, and depriving the community, in many cases, of the good that would come from the use of great tracts of agricultural land that are now held for speculative purposes;

Lack of good highway facilities;

The widespread continuing depletion of soils, with the injurious effect on rural life;

A general need of new and active leadership.

Other causes contributing to the general result are: Lack of any adequate system of agricultural credit, whereby the farmer may readily secure loans on fair terms; the shortage of labor, a condition that is often complicated by intemperance among workmen; lack of institutions and incentives that tie the laboring man to the soil; the burdens and the narrow life of farm women; lack of adequate supervision of public health.

The Nature of the Remedies.

Some of the remedies lie with the national Government, some of them with the States and communities in their corporate capacities, some with voluntary organizations, and some with individuals acting alone. From the great number of suggestions that have been made, covering every phase of country life, the Commission now enumerates those that seem to be most fundamental or most needed at the present time.

Congress can remove some of the handicaps of the farmer, and it can also set some kinds of work in motion, such as:

The encouragement of a system of thor-

oughgoing surveys of all agricultural regions
in order to take stock and to collect local
fact, with the idea of providing a basis on
which to develop a scientifically and economically sound country life;

The encouragement of a system of extension work in rural communities through
all the land-grant colleges with the people
at their homes and on their farms;

A thoroughgoing investigation by experts
of the middleman system of handling farm
products, coupled with a general inquiry
into the farmer's disadvantages in respect to
taxation, transportation rates, coöperative
organizations and credit, and the general
business system;

An inquiry into the control and use of the
streams of the United States with the object
of protecting the people in their ownership
and of saving to agricultural uses such
benefits as should be reserved for these
purposes;

The establishing of a highway engineering
service, or equivalent organization, to be at
the call of the states in working out effective
and economical highway systems;

The establishing of a system of parcels
posts and postal savings banks;

And providing some means or agency for

the guidance of public opinion toward the development of a real rural society that shall rest directly on the land.

Other remedies recommended for consideration by Congress are:

The enlargement of the United States Bureau of Education, to enable it to stimulate and coördinate the educational work of the nation;

Careful attention to the farmers' interests in legislation on the tariff, on regulation of railroads, control of regulation of corporations and of speculation, legislation in respect to rivers, forests and the utilization of swamp lands;

Increasing the powers of the federal government in respect to the supervision and control of the public health;

Providing such regulations as will enable the states that do not permit the sale of liquors to protect themselves from traffic from adjoining states.

In setting all these forces in motion, the coöperation of the States will be necessary; and in many cases definite state laws may greatly aid the work.

Remedies of a more general nature are: A

broad campaign of publicity, that must be undertaken until all the people are informed on the whole subject of rural life, and until there is an awakened appreciation of the necessity of giving this phase of our national development as much attention as has been given to other phases or interests; a quickened sense of responsibility in all country people, to the community and to the state in the conserving of soil fertility, and in the necessity for diversifying farming in order to conserve this fertility and to develop a better rural society, and also in the better safeguarding of the strength and happiness of the farm women; a more widespread conviction of the necessity for organization, not only for economic but for social purposes, this organization to be more or less coöperative, so that all the people may share equally in the benefits and have voice in the essential affairs of the community; a realization on the part of the farmer that he has a distinct natural responsibility toward the laborer in providing him with good living facilities and in helping him in every way to be a man among men; and a realization on the part of all the people of the obligation to protect and develop the natural scenery and attractiveness of the open country.

Certain remedies lie with voluntary organizations and institutions. All organized forces both in town and country should understand that there are country phases as well as city phases of our civilization, and that one phase needs help as much as the other. All these agencies should recognize their responsibility to society. Many existing organizations and institutions might become practically coöperative or mutual in spirit, as, for example, all agricultural societies, libraries, Young Men's Christian Associations and churches. All the organizations standing for rural progress should be federated, in states and nation.

THE UNDERLYING PROBLEM OF COUNTRY LIFE.

The mere enumeration of the foregoing deficiencies and remedies indicates that the problem of country life is one of reconstruction, and that temporary measures and defense work alone will not solve it. The underlying problem is to develop and maintain on our farms a civilization in full harmony with the best American ideals. To build up and retain this civilization means, first of all, that the business of agriculture must be made to yield a reasonable return to those who follow it intelligently; and life on the farm must be made permanently satisfying to intelligent, progressive people. The work before us, therefore, is nothing more or less than the gradual rebuilding of a new agriculture and new rural

life. We regard it as absolutely essential that
this great general work should be understood
by all the people. Separate difficulties, important
as they are, must be studied and worked out in
the light of the greater fundamental problem.

The Commission has pointed out a number of
remedies that are extremely important. But
running through all of these remedies are several
great forces, or principles, which must be utilized
in the endeavor to solve the problems of country
life. All the people should recognize what these
fundamental forces and agencies are.

Knowledge.—To improve any situation, the
underlying facts must be understood. The farmer
must have exact knowledge of his business and
of the particular conditions under which he
works. The United States Department of Agriculture and the experiment stations and colleges
are rapidly acquiring and distributing this knowledge; but the farmer may not be able to apply
it to the best advantage because of lack of
knowledge of his own soils, climate, animal and
plant diseases, markets, and other local facts.
The farmer is entitled to know what are the
advantages and disadvantages of his conditions
and environment. A thoroughgoing system of
surveys in detail of the exact conditions underlying farming in every locality is now an indis-

pensable need to complete and apply the work of the great agricultural institutions. As an occupation, agriculture is a means of developing our internal resources; we cannot develop these resources until we know exactly what they are.

Education.—There must be not only a fuller scheme of public education, but a new kind of education adapted to the real needs of the farming people. The country schools are to be so redirected that they shall educate their pupils in terms of the daily life. Opportunities for training toward agricultural callings are to be multiplied and made broadly effective. Every person on the land, old or young, in school or out of school, educated or illiterate, must have a chance to receive the information necessary for a successful business, and for a healthful, comfortable resourceful life, both in home and neighborhood. This means redoubled efforts for better country schools, and a vastly increased interest in the welfare of country boys and girls on the part of those who pay the school taxes. Education by means of agriculture is to be a part of our regular public school work. Special agricultural schools are to be organized. There is to be a well-developed plan of extension teaching conducted by the agricultural colleges, by means of the printed page, face-to-face talks, and demonstra-

tion or object lessons, designed to reach every
farmer and his family, at or near their homes,
with knowledge and stimulus in every department
of country life.

Organization.—There must be a vast enlargement of voluntary organized effort among farmers
themselves. It is indispensable that farmers shall
work together for their common interests and for
the national welfare. If they do not do this, no
governmental activity, no legislation, not even
better schools, will greatly avail. Much has been
done. There is a multitude of clubs, and association for social, educational and business purposes;
and great national organizations are effective.
But the farmers are nevertheless relatively unorganized. We have only begun to develop business coöperation in America. Farmers do not
influence legislation as they should. They need
a more fully organized social and recreative life.

Spiritual forces.—The forces and institutions
that make for morality and spiritual ideals among
rural people must be energized. We miss the
heart of the problem if we neglect to foster personal character and neighborhood righteousness.
The best way to preserve ideals for private conduct and public life is to build up the institutions
of religion. The church has great power of leadership. The whole people should understand that

it is vitally important to stand behind the rural church and to help it to become a great power in developing concrete country life ideals. It is especially important that the country church recognize that it has a social responsibility to the entire community as well as a religious responsibility to its own group of people.

Recommendations of the Commission

The Commission recommends all the correctives that have been mentioned under the head of " The Nature of the Remedies." It does not wish to discriminate between important measures of relief for existing conditions. It has purposely avoided endorsing any particular bill now before Congress, no matter what its value or object.

There are, however, in the opinion of the Commission, two or three great movements of the utmost consequence that should be set under way at the earliest possible time because they are fundamental to the whole problem of ultimate permanent reconstruction; these call for special explanation.

1. Taking stock of country life.—There should be organized, as explained in the main Report, under government leadership, a comprehensive plan for an exhaustive study or survey of all the conditions that surround the business of farming

and the people who live in the country, in order
to take stock of our resources and to supply
the farmer with local knowledge. Federal and
state governments, agricultural colleges and other
educational agencies, organizations of various
types, and individual students of the problem,
should be brought into coöperation for this great
work of investigating with minute care all agricultural and country life conditions.

2. Nationalized extension work.—Each state
college of agriculture should be empowered to
organize as soon as practicable, a complete
department of college extension, so managed as
to reach every person on the land in its state,
with both information and inspiration. The work
should include such forms of extension teaching as lectures, bulletins, reading-courses, correspondence courses, demonstration and other
means of reaching the people at home and on
their farms. It should be designed to forward
not only the business of agriculture, but sanitation, education, home-making, and all interests
of country life.

3. A campaign for rural progress.—We urge
the holding of local, state and even national
conferences on rural progress, designed to unite
the interests of education, organization and
religion into one forward movement for the

rebuilding of country life. Rural teachers, librarians, clergymen, editors, physicians and others may well unite with farmers in studying and discussing the rural question in all its aspects. We must in some way unite all institutions, all organizations, all individuals, having any interest in country life into one great campaign for rural progress.

THE CALL FOR LEADERSHIP.

We must picture to ourselves a new rural social structure, developed from the strong resident forces of the open country; and then we must set at work all the agencies that will tend to bring this about. The entire people need to be roused to this avenue of usefulness. Most of the new leaders must be farmers who can find not only a satisfying business career on the farm, but who will throw themselves into the service of upbuilding the community. A new race of teachers is also to appear in the country. A new rural clergy is to be trained. These leaders will see the great underlying problem of country life, and together they will work, each in his own field, for the one goal of a new and permanent rural civilization. Upon the development of this distinctively rural civilization rests ultimately our ability, by methods of farming requiring the highest intelligence, to continue to feed and clothe the hungry nations; to supply the city and metropolis with fresh blood, clean bodies and clear brains that can endure the strain of modern urban life; and to preserve a race of men in the open country that, in the future as in the past, will be the stay and strength of the nation in time of war, and its guiding and controlling spirit in time of peace.

It is to be hoped that many young men and women, fresh from our schools and institutions of learning, and quick with ambition and trained intelligence, will feel a new and strong call to service.

FULL REPORT OF THE COMMISSION

I

GENERAL STATEMENT

Broadly speaking, agriculture in the United States is prosperous and the conditions in many of the great farming regions are improving. The success of the owners and cultivators of good land, in the prosperous regions, has been due partly to improved methods, largely to good prices for products, and also to the general advance in the price of farm lands in these regions. Notwithstanding the general advance in rentals and the higher prices of labor, tenants also have enjoyed a good degree of prosperity, due to fair crops, and an advance in the price of farm products approximately corresponding to the advance in the price of land. Farm labor has been fully employed and at increased wages; and many farm hands have become tenants and many tenants have become landowners.

There is marked improvement, in many of the agricultural regions, in the character of the farm home and its surroundings. There is increasing appreciation on the part of great numbers of country people of the advantage of sanitary water supplies and plumbing, of better construction in barns and all farm buildings, of good reading matter, of tasteful gardens and lawns, and the necessity of good education.

Many institutions are also serving the agricultural needs of the open country with great effectiveness, as the United States Department of Agriculture, the land-grant colleges and experiment stations, and the many kinds of extension work that directly or indirectly emanate from them. The help that these institutions render to the country life interests is everywhere recognized. State departments of agriculture, national, state, and local organizations, many schools of secondary grade, churches, libraries, and many other agencies, are also contributing actively to the betterment of agricultural conditions.

There has never been a time when the American farmer was as well off as he is today, when we consider not only his earning power, but the comforts and advantages he may secure. Yet the real efficiency in farm life, and in country life as a whole, is not to be measured by historical standards, but in terms of its possibilities. Considered from this point of view, there are very marked deficiencies. There has been a complete and fundamental change in our whole economic system within the past century. This has resulted in profound social changes, and the redirection of our point of view on life. In some occupations, the readjustment to the new conditions has been rapid and complete; in others it has come with difficulty. In all the great series of farm occupations the readjustment has been the most tardy, because the whole structure of a traditional and fundamental system has been involved. It is not strange, therefore, that development is still arrested in certain respects, that marked inequalities have arisen, or that positive injustice may prevail even to a very marked and widespread extent. All these difficulties are the results of the unequal development of our contemporary civilization. All this may come about without any intention on the part of any one that it should be so. The problems are nevertheless just as real, and they must be studied and remedies must be found.

These deficiencies are recognized by the people. We have found, not only by the testimony of the farmers themselves, but of all persons in touch with farm life, more or less serious agricultural unrest in every part of the United States, even in the most prosperous regions. There is a widespread tendency for farmers to move to town. It is not advisable, of course, that all country persons remain in the country; but this general desire to move is evidence that the open country is not satisfying as a permanent abode. This tendency is not peculiar to any region. In difficult farming regions, and where the competition with other farming sections is most severe, the young people may go to town to better their condition. In the best regions, the older people retire to town because it is socially more attractive, and they see a prospect of living in comparative ease and comfort on the rental of their lands. Nearly everywhere there is a townward movement for the purpose of securing school advantages for the children. All this tends to sterilize the open country and to lower its social status. Often the farm is let to tenants. The farmer is likely to lose active interest in life when he retires to town, and he becomes a stationary citizen, adding a social problem to the town. He is likely to find his expenses increasing and is obliged to raise rents to his tenant, thereby making it more difficult for the man who works on the land. On his death his property enriches the town rather than the country. The withdrawal of the children from the farms detracts from the interest and efficiency of the country school and adds to the interest of the town school. Thus the country is drained of the energy of youth on the one hand, and the experience and accumulation of age on the other, and three problems more or less grave are created: a problem for the town, a problem for the public school, and also a problem of tenancy in the open country.

The farming interest is not as a whole receiving the full rewards to which it is entitled, nor has country life attained to anywhere near its possibilities of attractiveness and comfort. The farmer is necessarily handicapped in the development of social life and in the conduct of his business because of his separateness, the small volume of his output, and the lack of capital. He often begins with practically no capital, and expects to develop his capital and relationships out of the annual business itself; and even when he has capital with which to set up a business and operate it, the amount is small when compared with that required in other enterprises. He is not only handicapped in his farming, but is disadvantaged when he deals with other business interests and with other social groups. It is peculiarly necessary, therefore, that government should give him adequate consideration and protection. There are difficulties of the separate man, living quietly on his land, that government should understand.

THE PURPOSE OF THE COMMISSION.

The Commission is requested to report on the means that are "now available for supplying the deficiencies which exist" in the country life of the United States, and "upon the best methods of organized permanent effort in investigation and actual work" along the lines of betterment of rural conditions.

The President's letter appointing the Commission is as follows:

THE WHITE HOUSE
WASHINGTON

OYSTER BAY, N. Y.,
August 10, 1908.

My dear Professor Bailey:

No nation has ever achieved permanent greatness
unless this greatness was based on the well-being of
the great farmer class, the men who live on the soil;
for it is upon their welfare, material and moral, that
the welfare of the rest of the nation ultimately rests.
In the United States, disregarding certain sections and
taking the nation as a whole, I believe it to be true
that the farmers in general are better off today than
they ever were before. We Americans are making
great progress in the development of our agricultural
resources. But it is equally true that the social and
economic institutions of the open country are not
keeping pace with the development of the nation as
a whole. The farmer is, as a rule, better off than his
forebears; but his increase in well-being has not kept
pace with that of the country as a whole. While the
condition of the farmers in some of our best farming
regions leaves little to be desired, we are far from
having reached so high a level in all parts of the
country. In portions of the South, for example,
where the Department of Agriculture, through the
farmers' coöperative demonstration work of Doctor
Knapp, is directly instructing more than thirty thou-
sand farmers in better methods of farming, there is
nevertheless much unnecessary suffering and need-
less loss of efficiency on the farm. A physician, who

is also a careful student of farm life in the South, writing to me recently about the enormous percentage of preventable deaths of children due to the unsanitary condition of Southern farms, said:

> "Personally, from the health point of view, I would prefer to see my own daughter, nine years old, at work in a cotton mill, than have her live as tenant on the average Southern tenant one-horse farm. This apparently extreme statement is based upon actual life among both classes of people."

I doubt if any other nation can bear comparison with our own in the amount of attention given by the government, both federal and state, to agricultural matters. But practically the whole of this effort has hitherto been directed toward increasing the production of crops. Our attention has been concentrated almost exclusively on getting better farming. In the beginning this was unquestionably the right thing to do. The farmer must first of all grow good crops in order to support himself and his family. But when this has been secured, the effort for better farming should cease to stand alone, and should be accompanied by the effort for better business and better living on the farm. It is at least as important that the farmer should get the largest possible return in money, comfort, and social advantages from the crops he grows, as that he should get the largest possible return in crops from the land he farms. Agriculture is not the whole of country life.

The great rural interests are human interests, and good crops are of little value to the farmer unless they open the door to a good kind of life on the farm.

This problem of country life is in the truest sense a national problem. In an address delivered at the Semi-Centennial of the Founding of Agricultural Colleges in the United States a year ago last May, I said:

> "There is but one person whose welfare is as vital to the welfare of the whole country as is that of the wageworker who does manual labor; and that is the tiller of the soil—the farmer. If there is one lesson taught by history it is that the permanent greatness of any state must ultimately depend more upon the character of its country population than upon anything else. No growth of cities, no growth of wealth, can make up for loss in either the number or the character of the farming population.

> *   *   *   *   *

> "The farm grows the raw material for the food and clothing of all our citizens; it supports directly almost half of them; and nearly half the children of the Unites States are born and brought up on the farms. How can the life of the farm family be made less solitary, fuller of opportunity, freer from drudgery, more comfortable, happier, and more attractive? Such a result is most earnestly to be desired. How can life on the farm be kept on the highest level,

and where it is not already on that level, be so improved, dignified and brightened as to awaken and keep alive the pride and loyalty of the farmer's boys and girls, of the farmer's wife, and of the farmer himself? How can a compelling desire to live on the farm be aroused in the children that are born on the farm? All these questions are of vital importance not only to the farmer, but to the whole nation.

*   *   *   *   *

"We hope ultimately to double the average yield of wheat and corn per acre; it will be a great achievement; but it is even more important to double the desirability, comfort, and standing of the farmer's life."

It is especially important that whatever will serve to prepare country children for life on the farm, and whatever will brighten home life in the country and make it richer and more attractive for the mothers, wives and daughters of farmers should be done promptly, thoroughly and gladly. There is no more important person, measured in influence upon the life of the nation, than the farmer's wife, no more important home than the country home, and it is of national importance to do the best we can for both.

The farmers have hitherto had less than their full share of public attention along the lines of business and social life. There is too much belief among all our people that the prizes of life lie away from the farm. I am therefore anxious to bring before the people of the United States the question of securing better business and better living on the farm, whether by coöperation between farmers for buying, selling and borrowing; by promoting social advantages and opportunities in the country; or by any other legitimate means that will help to make country life more gainful, more attractive, and fuller of opportunities, pleasures and rewards for the men, women and children of the farms.

I shall be very glad indeed if you will consent to serve upon a Commission on Country Life, upon which I am asking the following gentlemen to act:

Professor L. H. Bailey, New York State College of Agriculture, Ithaca, N. Y., Chairman.

Mr. Henry Wallace, *Wallaces' Farmer*, Des Moines, Iowa.

President Kenyon L. Butterfield, Massachusetts Agricultural College, Amherst, Massachusetts.

Mr. Gifford Pinchot, United States Forest Service.

Mr. Walter H. Page, Editor of *The World's Work*, New York.

My immediate purpose in appointing this Commission is to secure from it such information and advice as will enable me to make recommendations to Congress upon this extremely important matter. I shall be glad if the Commission will report to me upon the present condition of country life, upon what means are now available for supplying the deficiencies which exist, and upon the best methods of organized permanent effort in investigation and actual work along the lines I have indicated. You will doubtless also find it necessary to suggest means for bringing about the redirection or better adaptation of rural schools to the training of children for life on the farm. The national and state agricultural departments must ultimately join with the various farmers' and agricultural organizations in the effort to secure greater efficiency and attractiveness in country life.

In view of the pressing importance of this subject, I should be glad to have you report before the end of next December. For that reason the Commission will doubtless find it impracticable to undertake extensive investigations, but will rather confine itself to a summary of what is already known, a statement of the problem, and the recommendation of measures tending towards its solution. With the single exception of the conservation of our natural resources, which underlies the problem of rural life, there is no other material question of greater importance now before the American people. I shall look forward with the keenest interest to your report.

Sincerely yours,

THEODORE ROOSEVELT.

Professor L. H. Bailey,
    New York State College of Agriculture,
        Ithaca, N. Y.

Subsequently, Charles S. Barrett of Georgia, and William A. Beard of California were added to the Commission.

The means that may be suggested for amelioration of country life fall under one or more of three general classes: (a) definite recommendations for executive or legislative action by the federal government; (b) suggestions for legislative enactment on the part of states; (c) suggestions or recommendations to the public at large as to what the Commission thinks would be the most fruitful lines of action and policy on the part of individuals, communities or states.

The problem before the Commission is to state, with some fulness of detail, the present conditions of country life, to point out the causes that may have led to its present lack of organization, to suggest methods by which it may be redirected, the drift to the city arrested, the natural rights of the farmer maintained, and an organized rural life developed that will promote the prosperity of the whole nation.

We are convinced that the forces that make for rural betterment must themselves be rural. We must arouse the country folk to the necessity for action, and suggest agencies which, when properly employed, will set them to work to develop a distinctly rural civilization.

In making its inquiries, the Commission has had constantly in mind the relation of the farmer to his community and to society in general. It has made no inquiry into problems of technical farming except as they may have bearing on general welfare and public questions.

The Commission has not assumed that country life conditions are either good or bad, nor is it within its province to compare country conditions with city conditions; but it has assumed that we have not yet arrived at that state of society in which conditions may not be bettered.

It is our place, therefore, to point out the deficiencies rather than the advantages and the progress. In doing this we must be distinctly understood as speaking only in general terms. The conditions that we describe do not, of course, apply equally in all parts of the country; and we have not been able to make studies of the problems of particular localities.

Before discussing the shortcomings more fully, we may explain how the Commission undertook its work.

METHODS PURSUED BY THE COMMISSION.

The field of inquiry has been the general social, economic, sanitary, educational and labor conditions of the open country. Within the time at its disposal, the Commission has not been able to make scientific investigations into any of these questions, but, following the suggestion of the President, has endeavored to give "a summary of what is already known, a statement of the problem, and the recommendation of measures looking towards its solution." We have been able to make a rather extensive exploration or reconnoissance of the field, to arrive at a judgment as to the main deficiencies of country life in the United States today, and to suggest some of the means of supplying these deficiencies.

The Commission and its work have met with the fullest coöperation and confidence on the part of the farmers and others, and the interest in the subject has been widespread. The people have been frank in giving information and expressing opinions, and in stating their problems and discouragements. There is every evidence that the people in rural districts have welcomed the Commission as an agency that is much needed

4

in the interest of country life, and in many of the hearings they have asked that the Commission be continued in order that it may make thorough investigations of the subjects that it has considered. The press has taken great interest in the work, and in many cases has been of special service to the Commission in securing direct information from country people.

The activities of the Commission have been directed mainly along four lines: the issuing of questions designed to bring out a statement of conditions in all parts of the United States; correspondence and inquiries by different members of the Commission, so far as time would permit, each in a particular field; the holding of hearings in many widely separated places; discussions in local meetings, held in response to a special suggestion by the President.[1]

---

[1] The President's suggestion for meetings in school houses and other local places is as follows (this letter was not included in the Report of the Commission.):

THE WHITE HOUSE, WASHINGTON,
November 9, 1908.

My dear Professor Bailey:

I wish at the outset cordially to thank you for the way in which you have taken hold of the work you are doing. No more valuable work for the people of this country can be done,

THE CIRCULAR OF QUESTIONS.

As a means of securing the opinions of the people themselves on some of the main aspects of country life, a set of questions was distributed, as follows:

    I. Are the farm homes in your neighborhood as good as they should be under existing conditions?

   II. Are the schools in your neighborhood training boys and girls satisfactorily for life on the farm?

 III. Do the farmers in your neighborhood get the returns they reasonably should from the sale of their products?

because no more valuable work for the farmers of this country can be done.

Now of course the whole success of the work depends upon the attitude of the people in the open country, of the farming people of the United States. If they feel an awakening interest in what you are doing, they should manifest it. Moreover, it is essential that the farmers, the men who actually live on the soil, should feel a sense of ownership in this Commission, should feel that you gentlemen in very truth represent them and are responsive to their desires and wishes, no less than to their needs. It seems to me, therefore, that it would be wise to try to get into the closest possible touch with the farmers of the country and to find out from them, so far as you are able, just what they regard as being the subjects with which it is most important that you should deal. This you are already doing by sending out a circular of questions and by holding meetings in different parts of the United States. But perhaps something more can be done.

I accordingly suggest that you ask the farmers to come together in the several school districts of the country so that they

IV. Do the farmers in your neighborhood receive from the railroads, highroads, trolley lines, etc., the services they reasonably should have?

V. Do the farmers in your neighborhood receive from the United States postal service, rural telephones, etc., the service they reasonably should expect?

VI. Are the farmers and their wives in your neighborhood satisfactorily organized to promote their mutual buying and selling interest?

VII. Are the renters of farms in your neighborhood making a satisfactory living?

VIII. Is the supply of farm labor in your neighborhood satisfactory?

IX. Are the conditions surrounding hired labor on the farms in your neighborhood satisfactory to the hired man?

may meet and consider these matters. I suggest the school districts because the school house would be the natural and proper place for such a meeting; or they could meet at other customary or convenient places. It would be well if the meetings could be held within the next three or four weeks; that is, before Congress adjourns prior to the Christmas holidays, so that at the time of the reassembling of Congress early in January you will have the reports of the meetings and so will be in position to advise definitely what should be done. I suggest that you ask them to meet, not later than Saturday, December 5th; and you will, of course, use your own judgment whether to summon the meeting by circular or otherwise.

Thruout this letter where I use the word "farmers" I mean also to include all those who live in the open country and are intimately connected with those who do the farm work—ministers, school teachers, physicians, editors of country papers, in

    X. Have the farmers in your neighborhood satisfactory facilities for doing their business in banking, credit, insurance, etc.?

    XI. Are the sanitary conditions of farms in your neighborhood satisfactory?

    XII. Do the farmers and their wives and families in your neighborhood get together for mutual improvement, entertainment and social intercourse as much as they should?

What, in your judgment, is the most important single thing to be done for the general betterment of country life?

Note: Following each question are the sub-questions:

    a. Why?

    b. What suggestions have you to make?

---

short, all men and women whose life work is done either on the farm or in connection with the life work of those who are on the farm.

You know better than I what topics you will suggest. How would it do to include such topics as:

    The efficiency of the rural schools;
    Farmers' organizations;
    The question of farm labor;
    The need of good roads;
    Improved postal facilities;
    Sanitary conditions on the farm.

Your purpose is neither to investigate the farmer, nor to inquire into technical methods of farming. You are simply trying to ascertain what are the general economic, social, educational and sanitary conditions of the open country, and what, if anything, the farmers themselves can do to help themselves, and how the Government can help them. To this end your especial

About 550,000 copies of the circular questions were sent to names supplied by the United States Department of Agriculture, state experiment stations, farmers' societies, women's clubs, to rural free deliverymen, country physicians and ministers, and others. To these inquiries about 115,000 persons have now replied, mostly with much care and with every evidence of good faith. Nearly 100,000 of these circulars have been ar-

---

desire is to get in touch with and represent the farmers themselves. The Commission now consists of five members. I shall ask two more gentlemen to serve upon it, so that the full membership will be as follows:

Professor L. H. Bailey, New York State College of Agriculture, Ithaca, N. Y., Chairman;

Mr. Henry Wallace, *Wallaces' Farmer:* Des Moines, Iowa;

Kenyon L. Butterfield, President Massachusetts Agricultural College, Amherst, Mass.;

Gifford Pinchot, U. S. Forest Service, Washington, D. C.;

Walter H. Page, of North Carolina, Editor of *The World's Work*;

Charles S. Barrett, Union City, Ga., and

William A. Beard, Sacramento, Cal.

Again thanking you, and with all good wishes for your success in this great and important work, believe me,

Very sincerely yours,

THEODORE ROOSEVELT.

Professor L. H. Bailey, Chairman,
  Commission on Country Life,
    New York State College of Agriculture,
      Ithaca, New York.

ranged and some of the information tabulated in a preliminary way by the Census Bureau. In addition to the replies to the circulars, great numbers of letters and carefully written statements have been received, making altogether an invaluable body of information, opinion and suggestion.

THE HEARINGS.

Hearings were held at thirty places by the whole Commission, or part of it, between November 9 and December 22, 1908; and frequently two or more long sessions were held. Very full notes were taken of the proceedings. They were attended by good audiences, in some instances overflowing the hall. At several, especially in the Northwest, delegates were in attendance representing associations and communities in the vicinity, who were anxious to present their views and needs. Speeches were numerous and usually short and pithy, and represented every sort of person concerned with rural life, including many women, who contributed much to the domestic and educational aspects of the subject. The governors and principal officials of the states

were often present; and also the presidents and
professors of institutions of learning, clergymen,
physicians, librarians, and others, but the bulk
of the speakers and audiences was country
people.   No attempt was made to follow a definite program of questioning, but general discussions proceeded, with an occasional show of
hands or outburst of applause to signify general
assent to the speaker's words.

The hearings were held as follows:

Nov. 9,   College Park, Md.
       10,   Richmond, Va.
       11,   Raleigh, N. C., and Athens, Ga.
       12,   Spartansburg, S. C.
       13,   Knoxville, Tenn.
       14,   Lexington, Ky.
       16–18, Washington, D. C.
       19–21, Dallas, Texas.
       22–23, El Paso, Texas.
       24,   Tucson, Ariz.
       25–26, Los Angeles, Cal.
       27–28, Fresno, Cal.
       28–29, San Francisco, Cal.
       30,   Sacramento, Cal.
Dec.   1,   Reno, Nevada.
       2,   Portland, Ore.
       4–5, Spokane, Wash., (and at Opportun-
             ity, near by).

Dec. 2–3, Salt Lake City, Utah.
    5, Cheyenne, Wyo.
    6, Bozeman, Mont.
    7–8, Denver, Col.
    9–10, Omaha, Neb.
    10, Council Bluffs, Ia.
    11, Minneapolis, Minn. (St. Anthony Park).
    12, Madison, Wis.
    14, Champaign, Ill.
    16, Ithaca, N. Y.
    17, Springfield, Mass.
    18, Boston, Mass.
    22, Washington, D. C.

THE SCHOOL-HOUSE MEETINGS.

The suggestion of the President that the country people of the United States come together in their district school-houses to discuss country life questions under consideration by the Commission, was officially transmitted by the Commission to the state and county superintendents of schools of every state and territory. A great part of the press of the country quoted the suggestion in full, often printing with it the original list of questions issued by the Commission. School officials, ministers of country churches and other persons concerned in the advancement of country matters, contributed their active efforts for organizing such meetings. Reports of meetings have already come in from almost every state, and we have notice of many meetings still to be held. Separate states have set specific days for simultaneous meetings in all their country school-houses, notably Nebraska and Missouri. The States of Washington, Oregon, Montana and Idaho by concerted arrangement held a meeting December 5, the date suggested by the President. Suggestion has come from many parts of the country for the regular establishment of such meetings for annual national observance by the country people as an inventory-taking day, and for planning community advancement for the ensuing year.

II

THE MAIN SPECIAL DEFICIENCES IN COUNTRY LIFE

The numbers of problems and suggestions that have been presented to the Commission in the hearings and through the correspondence are very great. We have chosen for special discussion those that are most significant and that seem most to call for immediate action. The main single deficiency is, of course, lack of the proper kind of education, but inasmuch as the redirection of educational methods is also the main remedy for the shortcomings of country life, as also of any other life, the discussion of it may be reserved for Part III.

1. DISREGARD OF THE INHERENT RIGHTS OF LAND-WORKERS.

Notwithstanding an almost universal recognition of the importance of agriculture to the maintenance of our people, there is nevertheless a widespread disregard of the rights of the men who own and work the land. This results directly in social depression as well as in economic disadvantage.

The organized and corporate interests represented in mining, manufacturing, merchandizing, transportation and the like, seem often to hold the idea that their business may be developed and exploited without regard to the farmers who should, however, have an equal opportunity for enjoyment of the land, forests and streams, and of the right to buy and sell in the open markets without prejudice.

The question of the moral intention of the consolidated interests is not involved in these statements. The present condition has grown up; and without going into the reasons, it is imperative that we recognize these disadvantages to country life interests and seek to correct them. The way in which discriminating conditions may arise is well illustrated in the inequalities of taxation of farm property. It is natural that visible and stationary property should be taxed freely under our present system; it is equally natural that invisible and changeable property should tend to evade taxation. The inevitable result is that the farmer's property bears an unjust part in taxation schemes.

Nor is this disregard of the inherent rights of the land-worker confined to corporations and companies, or to the recognized inequalities of taxation. It is often shared by cities. Instead of taking care of their own undesirables, they often turn them off on the country districts. The "fringe" of a city thereby becomes a low-class or even vicious community, and its influence often extends far into the country districts. The Commission hears complaints that hoboes are driven from the cities and towns into the country districts where there is no machinery for controlling them.

The subjects to which we are here inviting attention are, of course, not confined to country life alone. They express an attitude toward public questions in general. We look for the development of a sentiment that will protect and promote the welfare of all the people whenever there is a conflict with the interests of a small or particular class.

The handicaps that we now have specially in mind may be stated under four heads: Speculative holding of lands; monopolistic control of streams; wastage and monopolistic control of forests; restraint of trade.

(a) SPECULATIVE HOLDING OF LANDS.

Certain land-owners procure large areas of agricultural land in the most available location, sometimes by questionable methods, and hold it for speculative purposes. This not only withdraws the land itself from settlement, but in many cases prevents the development of an agricultural community. The smaller land-owners are isolated and unable to establish their necessary institutions or to attract the attention of the market. The holding of large areas by one party, tends to develop a system of tenantry and absentee farming. The whole development may be in the direction of social and economic ineffectiveness. In parts of the West and South, this evil is so pronounced that persons have requested the Commission to recommend measures of relief by restricting, under law, the size of speculative holdings of agricultural lands.

A similar problem arises in respect to the utilization of the swamp lands of the United States.

According to the reports of the United States Geological Survey, there are more than seventy-five million acres of swamp land in this country, the greater part of which are capable of reclamation at probably a nominal cost as compared to their value. It is important to the development of the best type of country life that the reclamation of the lands in rural regions proceed under conditions insuring their subdivision into small farm units and their settlement by men who would both own them and till them. Some of these lands are near the centers of population. They become a menace to health, and they often prevent the development of good social conditions in very large areas of country. As a rule, they are extremely fertile. They are capable of sustaining an agricultural population numbering many millions; and the conditions under which these millions must live are properly a matter of national concern. In view of these facts, the federal government should act to the fullest extent of its constitutional powers in securing the reclamation of these lands under proper safeguards against speculative holding and landlordism. It may be that in the case of those lands ceded to the states for the purpose of reclamation, the greater part of which are unreclaimed, there exists a special authority on the part of the federal government by reason of failure to comply with the terms of the grant; and there should be a vigorous legal inquiry into the present rights of the government with respect to them, followed, if the status warrants it, by legal steps to rescind the grants and to begin the practical work of reclamation.

(b) MONOPOLISTIC CONTROL OF STREAMS.

The legitimate farming interests of the whole country would be vastly benefited by a systematic conservation and utilization, under the auspices of the state and federal governments, of our waterways both great and small. Important advantages of these waterways are likely to be appropriated in perpetuity and without adequate return to the people by monopolistic interests that deprive the permanent agricultural inhabitants of the use of them.

The rivers are valuable to the farmers as drainage lines, as sources of irrigation supply, as carriers and equalizers of transportation rates, as a readily available power resource, and for the raising of food fish. The wise development of these and other uses is important to both agricultural and other interests; their protection from monopoly is one of the first responsibilities of government. The streams belong to the people; under a proper system of development their resources would remain an estate of all the people, and become available as needed. A broad constructive program involving coördinate development of the many uses of streams, under conditions insuring their permanent control in the interest of the people themselves, is urgently needed, and none should be more concerned in this than the farmers.

River navigation affords the best and cheapest transportation of farm products of a non-perishable nature. The rivers afford the best means of competition with railroads, because river carriage is cheap, and because the rivers once opened by the government for navigation are open to all and monopoly of their use should be an impossibility. Interest in river improvement for the purpose of navigation is very keen among the farmers who actually use river transportation, and to some extent among farmers who enjoy

5

advantages in railway rates due to parallel water lines; but the great mass of farmers, while complaining of what they affirm to be unjust and exhorbitant railway rates, have given too little thought to the means of relief with which nature has favored them. This is probably due to lack of knowledge of the actual economies of river transportation. For example, one community located 200 miles from a former head of navigation, ships wheat by rail to a market that is 1,033 miles distant, at a cost of 21 cents per bushel, yet it showed no interest in the reopening of the channel that would reduce the train haul to less than one fifth the distance.

This failure to consider the waterways is probably due very largely to the high rates per ton mile charged by railroads for short hauls. Under the present methods of fixing the railway tariffs, local rates are often almost or quite as great as between points far distant, and there is small inducement to use cheap river freights because of the cost of reaching the river banks. The remedy for this lies in two directions: It must come either from a rearrangement of freight schedules, which may involve a complete change in the present policy of the railway companies with reference thereto; or by means of competition by independent or local companies.

It must be remembered, also, that no interests inimical to the public welfare should be allowed to acquire permanent control of the stream banks. Facilities for ready and economical approach are practically as important as the channels themselves.

River transportation is not usually antagonistic to railway interests. Population and production are increasing rapidly, with corresponding increase in the demands made on transportation facilities. It may be reasonably expected that in the evolution of the transportation business, the rivers will eventually carry a large part of the freight that does not require prompt delivery, while the railways will carry that requiring expeditious handling. This is already foreseen by leading railway men; and its importance to the farmer is such that he should encourage and aid, by every means in his power, the movement for large use of the rivers. The country will produce enough business to tax both streams and railroads to their utmost.

In many regions the streams afford facilities for the development of power, which, since the successful inauguration of electrical transmission, is available for local rail lines and offers the best solution of local transportation problems. In many parts of the country, local and interurban lines are providing transportation to farm areas, thereby increasing the facilities for moving crops and adding to the profit and convenience of farm life. Notwithstanding this development, however, there seems to be a very general lack of appreciation, on the part of farmers, of the possibilities of this water-power resource as a factor in governing transportation costs.

The streams may also be used as a source of small water power on thousands of farms. This is particularly true of the small streams. Much of the manual labor about the house and barn can be performed from transmission of power from small water-wheels running on the farms themselves or in the neighborhood. This power could be used for electric lighting and for small manufacture. It is more important that small power be developed on the farms of the United States than that we harness Niagara.

Unfortunately, the tendency of the present laws is to encourage the acquisition of these resources on easy terms or on their own terms by the first applicants, and the power of the streams is rapidly being acquired under conditions that lead to the concentration of ownership in the hands of monopolies. This state of things constitutes a real and immediate danger, not to the country life interests alone, but to the entire nation, and it is time that the whole people become aroused to it.

The laws under which water is appropriated or flowage rights secured for power were enacted prior to the introduction of electrical transmission, and, consequently, before there was any possibility of water power becoming of more than local importance or value. Monopoly of water power was practically impossible while the sources and uses were alike isolated, but the present ability to concentrate the power of streams and to develop transportation, manufacturing, heating, and lighting on a vast scale invites monopolization.

It appears as a result of governmental investigation that practically in the last five years there has been a very significant concentration of water powers; that this concentration has now placed about 33 per cent of the total developed water powers of the country under the control of a group of thirteen companies or interests; that there are very strong economic and technical reasons forcing such concentration. The rapid concentration already accomplished, together with the obvious technical reasons for further control and the financial advantages to be gained by a substantial monopoly, justifies the fear that the concentration already accomplished is but the forerunner of a far greater degree of monopoly of water power. Unless the people become aroused to the danger to their interests, there will probably be developed a monopoly greater than any the world has yet seen.

The development of power plants and of industries using this power ought to be encouraged by every legitimate and proper means. It should not be necessary, however, to grant perpetual rights in order to encourage this development. There should be no perpetual grant of water power privileges. On the contrary, the ownership of the people should be perpetually maintained, and grants should be in the nature of terminable franchises.

The irrigation water should be protected. Farm life in the irrigated regions is usually of an advanced type, due principally to the small size of farms and the resulting social and educational advantages, and to intensive agriculture. Because of these facts, the development of the arid regions by irrigation may be a distinct contribution to the improvement of the country life of the nation. In the use of streams for irrigation, as in other uses, monopoly should be discouraged. The ownership of water for irrigation is no less important than the ownership of land; water-lordism is as much to be feared as landlordism. In the irrigated regions, the water is more valuable than the land to which it is applied; the availability of the water supply often gives to the land all the value that it has, and when this is true it must follow that the farmer must own both the water and the land if he is to be master of his own fortunes. One of the very best elements of any population is the independent home-owning farmer, and the tendency of government, so far as may be practicable, should be towards securing the ownership of the land by the man who lives on it and tills it. It should seek to vest in the farmer of the irrigated region the title to his water supply and to protect his tenure of it. The national reclamation act under which large areas of arid land are now being placed under irrigation, is commended as a contribution to the development of a good country life in the West, not alone because it renders available for settlement large areas of previously worthless land, but still more because it insures to settlers the ownership of both the land and the water.

The need to utilize the streams is to be considered in the East as well as in the West.

The Commission suggests that a special inquiry be made of the control of stream resources of the United States, with the object of protecting the people in their ownership and of reserving to agricultural uses such benefits as should be reserved for these purposes.

(c) WASTAGE AND CONTROL OF FORESTS.

The forests have been exploited for private gain until not only has the timber been seriously reduced, but until streams have been ruined for navigation, power, irrigation and common water supplies and whole regions have been exposed to floods and disastrous soil erosion. Probably there has never occurred a more reckless destruction of property that of right should belong to all the people. These devastations are checked on the government lands, but similar devastation in other parts of the country is equally in need of attention. The Commission has heard strong demands from farmers for the establishment of forest reservations in the White Mountains and the southern Appalachian region, to save the timber and to control the sources of streams, and no statements in opposition to the proposal. Measures should be enacted creating such reservations. The forests as well as the streams should be saved from monopolistic control.

The conservation of forests and brush on watershed areas is important to the farmer along the full length of streams regardless of the distance between the farm and these areas. The loss of soil in denuded areas increases the menace of flood, not alone because of the more rapid run-off, but by the filling of channels and the greater erosion of stream banks when soil matter is carried in suspension.

Loss of soil by washing is a serious menace to the fertility of the American farm. A high authority on this subject recently made the statement that soil wash is "the heaviest impost borne by the American farmer."

The wood-lot property of the country needs to be saved and increased. Wood-lot yield is one of the most important crops of the farm, and is of great value to the public in controlling streams, saving the run-off, checking winds, and in adding to the attractiveness of the region. In many regions, where poor and hilly lands prevail, the town or county could well afford to purchase forest land, expecting thereby to add to the value of the property and eventually to make the forests a source of revenue. Such communal forests in Europe yield revenue to the cities and towns by which they are owned and managed.

(d) RESTRAINT OF TRADE.

The Commission has heard much complaint, in all parts of the country and by all classes of farmers, of injustice, inequalities and discrimination on the part of transportation companies and middlemen. These are the most universal direct complaints that have been presented to the Commission. If the statements can be trusted, the business of farming as a whole is greatly repressed by lack of mutual understanding and good faith in the transportation and marketing of agricultural produce.

Without expressing an opinion on these questions, we feel that there should be a free understanding between transportation companies and farmers in respect to their mutual business. We find that farmers who have well-informed opinions on tariff, education and other public questions are yet wholly uninformed in respect to the transportation man's point of view on freight rates and express rates that may be in dispute. A disposition on the part of all parties to discuss the misunderstandings fairly would probably accomplish much.

The whole matter of railway freight rates should be made more understandable. There should be a simplifying or codifying of rates that will enable the farmer or a group of farmers or of other citizens who use the railways, to ascertain

readily from the published tariffs the actual rate
on any given commodity between two points.
Railway rate-making is fundamentally a matter
of public importance. The rates are a large factor
in the development of population; in many
instances the railway rates determine both the
character of the population and the development
of industry. The railway companies, by their
rates, may decide where the centers of distribution shall be, what areas shall develop manufactures and other special industries. To the extent
that they do this they exercise a purely public
function, and for this reason alone, if for no other,
the government should exercise a wise supervision over the making and publication of rates.
Favoritism to large shippers has been one of the
principal abuses of the transportation business
and has contributed to the growth of monopolies
of trade. While rebating is largely discontinued,
it is very generally believed that this favoritism
is still practiced, in various forms, to an entent
that works a hardship on the small shipper and
the unorganized interests. Complaint is not confined to steam roads alone but is directed towards
the trolley lines as well. There is a feeling that

trolley systems should be feeders to the steam roads, and that these systems which are rapidly being extended through rural districts should afford to farmers a freight service that is ready, rapid, and cheap. It is charged that this is not done, that steam lines discourage the use of the trolleys for freight, or absorb them and eliminate competition to the detriment of the farm population which they should most benefit.

The Interstate Commerce Commission exercises a most valuable governmental function. It is a body to which complaint may be made of any rate considered to be unreasonable. It has been of great benefit to the farmers of the country. What is needed now is a careful study of the railway situation with a veiw to reaching and correcting abuses and practices still in existence that operate against the unorganized and the rural interests.

In this connection, attention is invited to the fact that many states have railway commissions charged with the duty of protecting the public from paying exorbitant frieght rates, and farmers who feel that they are charged more than is fair should see to it, first, that their state railway commissions are composed of men who will do their duty; and, second, that these men are sustained in honest efforts to do their duty with fairness to all concerned. The charge is frequently made that these commissions are not effective, but as they are a part of the machinery of the state, it would seem that the farmers have here an excellent opportunity to serve their interests by active devotion to a plain political duty.

Dissatisfaction with the prevailing systems of marketing is very general. There is a widespread belief that certain middlemen consume a share of agricultural sales out of all proportion to the services they render, either to the consumer or the producer, making a larger profit—often without risk—in the selling of the product than the farmer makes in producing it. We have no desire to condemn middlemen as a class. We have no doubt that there are many businesses of this kind that are conducted on a square deal basis, but we are led to believe that grave abuses are practiced by unscrupulous persons and firms, and we recommend a searching inquiry into the methods employed in the sale of produce on commission.

(e) REMEDIES FOR THE DISREGARD OF THE INHER-
ENT RIGHTS OF THE FARMER.

We need, in the first place, as a people, to
recognize the necessary rights of the individual
farmer to the use of the native resources and
agencies that go with the utilization of agricultural lands, and to protect him from hindrance
and encroachment in the normal development
of his business. If the farmer suffers because his
business is small, isolated and unsyndicated,
then it is the part of government to see that he
has a natural opportunity among his fellows and
a square deal.

In the second place, we need such an attitude
of government, both state and national, as will
safeguard the separate and individual rights of
the farmer, in the interest of the public good. As
a contribution toward this attitude, we commend
the general policy of the present administration
to safeguard the streams, forests, coal lands, and
phosphate lands, and in endeavoring to develop
a home-owning settlement in the irrigated regions.

At the moment, one of the most available and
effective single means of giving the farmer the
benefit of his natural opportunities is the enlarge-

ment of government service to the country people through the post office. We hold that a parcels post and a postal savings bank system are necessities; and as rapidly as possible the rural free delivery of mails should be extended. Everywhere we have found the farmers demanding the parcels post. It is opposed by many merchants, transportation organizations and established interests. We do not think that the parcels post will injure the merchant in the small town or elsewhere. Whatever will permanently benefit the farmer will benefit the country as a whole. Both town and country would readjust themselves to the new conditions. We recognize the great value of the small town to the country districts and would not see it displaced or crippled; but the character of the open country largely makes or unmakes the country town.

In order that fundamental correctives may be applied, we recommend that a thoroughgoing study or investigation be made of the relation of business practices and of taxation to the welfare of the farmer, with a view to ascertaining what discriminations and deficiencies may exist, whether legislation is needed, and to give publicity to

the entire subject. This investigation should
include the entire middleman system, farmers'
coöperative organizations, transportation rates
and practices, taxation of agricultural property,
methods of securing funds on reasonable conditions for agricultural uses, and the entire range
of economic questions involved in the relation of
the farmer to the accustomed methods of doing
business.

We find that there is need of a new general
attitude toward legislation, in the way of safeguarding the farmers' natural rights and interests.
It is natural that the organized and consolidated
interests should be strongly in mind in the making
of legislation. We recommend that the welfare
of the farmer and countryman be also kept in
mind in the construction of laws. We specially
recommend that his interests be considered and
safeguarded in any new legislation on the tariff,
on regulation of railroads, control or regulating
of corporations and of speculation, river, swamp,
and forest legislation, and public health regulation.
At the present moment, it is especially important
that the farmer's interests be well considered in
the revision of the tariff. One of the particular

6

needs is such an application of the reciprocity
principle as to open European markets for our
flour, meats and live cattle.   One of the great
economic problems of our agriculture is how to
feed the corn crop and other grains profitably,
for it must be fed if the fertility of the land is to
be maintained; to dispose of the crop profitably
requires the best markets that can be secured.

2. Highways.

The demand for good highways is general
among the farmers of the entire United States.
Education and good roads are the two needs
most frequently mentioned in the hearings.
Highways that are usable at all times of the year
are now imperative, not only for the marketing
of produce, but for the elevation of the social
and intellectual status of the open country, and
the improvement of health by insuring better
medical and surgical attendance.

The advantages are so well understood that
arguments for better roads are not necessary here.
Our respondents are now concerned largely with
the methods of organizing and financing the work.
With only unimportant exceptions, the farmers

who have expressed themselves to us on this question consider that the federal government is fairly under obligation to aid in the work.

We hold that the development of a fully serviceable highway system is a matter of national concern, coördinate with the development of waterways and the conservation of our native resources. It is absolutely essential to our internal development. The first thing necessary is to provide expert supervision and direction, and to develop a national plan. All the work should be coöperative between the federal government and the states. The question of federal appropriation for highway work in the states may well be held in abeyance until a national service is provided and tested. We suggest that the United States government establish a highway engineering service, or equivalent organization, to be at the call of the states in working out effective and economical highway systems.

3. SOIL DEPLETION AND ITS EFFECTS.

A condition calling for serious comment is the lessening productiveness of the land. Our farming has been largely exploitational, consisting of mining the virgin fertility. On the better lands this primitive system of land exploitation may last for two generations without results pernicious to society, but on the poorer lands the limit of satisfactory living conditions may be reached in less than one generation.

The social condition of any agricultural community is closely related to the available fertility of the soil. " Poor land, poor people " and " Rough land, rough people," have long since passed into proverbs. Rich land well farmed does not necessarily mean high ideals or good society. It may mean land-greed and dollar-worship; but on the other hand, high ideals cannot be realized without at least a fair degree of prosperity, and this can not be secured without the maintenance of fertility.

When the land begins to yield with difficulty, the farmer may move to new land; develop a system of self-sustaining agriculture (becoming thereby a real farmer); or be driven into poverty and degradation. The first of these results has been marked for many years, but it is now greatly checked because most of the available lands have been occupied. The second result—

the evolution of a really scientific and self-perpetuating agriculture—is beginning to appear here and there, mostly in the long-settled regions. The drift to poverty and degradation is pronounced in many parts of the country. In every region a certain class of the population is forced to the poor lands, becoming a handicap to the community and constituting a very difficult social problem.

There are two great classes of farmers: those who make farming a real and active constructive business, as much as the successful manufacturer or merchant makes his effort a business; and those who merely passively live on the land, often because they cannot do anything else, and by dint of hard work and the strictest economy manage to subsist. Each class has its difficulties. The problems of the former class are largely those arising from the man's relation to the world at large. The farmer of the latter class is not only powerless as against trade in general, but is also more or less helpless in his own farming problems. In applying corrective measures, we must recognize these two classes of persons.

When no change of system has followed the

depletion of the virgin fertility, the saddest results have followed. The former owners have often lost the land and a system of tenantry farming has gradually developed. This is marked in all regions that are dominated by a one-crop system of agriculture. In parts of the Southern states this loss of available fertility is specially noticeable, particularly where cotton is the main if not the only crop. In some parts of the country this condition and the social results are pathetic, and particularly where the farmers, whether white or black, by reason of poverty and lack of credit and want of experience in other kinds of farming, are compelled to continue to grow cotton. Large numbers of Southern farmers are still obliged to mortgage their unplanted crop to secure the means of living while it is growing; and, as a matter of course, they pay exorbitant prices for the barest necessities of life. The only security that the man can give, either to the banker or the merchant, is cotton, and this forces the continued cultivation of a crop that decreases the soil fertility in a country of open winters where the waste by erosion is necessarily at the maximum. The tenants have little interest in the land and move from year to year in the vain hope of better luck. The average income of the tenant farmer family growing cotton is about $150 a year; and the family usually does not raise its poultry, meat, fruit, vegetables, or bread-stuffs. The landlords in large sections are little better off than the tenants. The price of the product is manipulated by speculators. The tenant farmer, and even the landlord, is preyed upon by other interests and is practically powerless. The effect of the social stratification into landlord, tenant, and money-lending merchant, still further complicates a situation that in some regions is desperate and that demands vigorous treatment.

The recent years of good prices for cotton have enabled many farmers to get out of debt and to be able to handle their own business. These farmers are then free to begin a new system of husbandry. The problems still remain, however, of how to help the man who is still in bondage.

While these conditions are specially marked in the cotton-growing states, they are arising in all regions of a single-crop system, except, perhaps, in the case of fruit regions and vegetable regions. They are beginning to appear in the exclusive wheat regions, where the yields are constantly growing less and where the social life is usually monotonous and barren. The hay-selling system of many parts of the Northeastern states presents similar results, as does also the exclusive corn-grownig for the general market when stock-raising is not a part of the business.

The loss of fertility in the Northern states is less rapid because of the climatic conditions that arrest the winter waste; fewer landlords, and these for the most part retired farmers who live near their farms and largely control the methods of cultivating the land; and a different kind of agriculture and a different social structure. It is, however, serious enough even in the Northern states, and especially in the Mississpipi Valley, particularly when lands are held as an investment by capitalists who know nothing about farming and care only for annual returns, and also when held by speculators in the hope of harvesting the unearned increment, which has been large of late years, due probably to some world-wide cause, which it is beyond our province to discuss. In any case, whether North or South, it has become a matter of very serious concern, whether farmers are to continue to dominate and direct the policy of the people as they do now in large part in the more prosperous agricultural sections, or whether, because of soil deterioration they shall become a dependent class or shall be tenants in name, but laborers in fact and working for an uncertain wage.

Fortunately there is abundant evidence on every hand, both North and South, that the fertility of the soil can be maintained, or where it has been greatly decreased can be restored at least approximately to its virgin fertility. The hope of the future lies in the work of the public institutions that are devoted to the new agriculture. The United States Department of Agriculture, experiment stations, colleges of agriculture and other agencies are making great progress in correcting these and other deficiencies, and these institutions deserve the sympathetic support of all the people. The demonstration work of the Department of Agriculture in the Southern states is a marked example of the good that can be done by teaching the people how to diversify their farming and to redeem themselves from the bondage of an hereditary system. Similar work is needed in many parts of the United States, and it is already under way, in various forms, under the leadership of the land-grant institutions.

The great agricultural need of the open country is a system of diversified and rotation farming, carefully adapted in every case to the particular region. Such systems conserve the resources of the land, and develop diversified and active institutions. Nor is this wastage of soil resources peculiar to one-crop systems, although it is more marked in such cases: it is a general feature of our agriculture due to a lack of appreciation of our responsibility to society to protect and save the land. Although we have reason to be proud of our agricultural achievements, we must not close our eyes to the fact that our soil resources are still being lost through poor farming.

This lessening of soil fertility is marked in every part of the United States, even in the richest lands of the prairies. It marks the pioneer stage of land usage. It has now become an acute national danger, and the economic, social and political problems arising out of it must at once receive the best attention of statesmen. The attention that has been given to these questions is wholly inadqeuate to the urgency of the dangers involved.

4. AGRICULTURAL LABOR.

There is a general, but not a universal, complaint of scarcity of farm labor. This scarcity is not an agricultural difficulty alone, but one phase or expression of the general labor supply problem.

So long as the United States continues to be a true democracy, it will have a serious labor problem. As a democracy, we honor labor, and the higher the efficiency of the labor, the greater the honor. The laborer, if he has the ambition to be an efficient agent in the development of the country, will be anxious to advance from the lower to the higher forms of effort, and from being a laborer himself he becomes a director of labor. If he has nothing but his hands and brains, he aims to accumulate sufficient capital to become a tenant, and eventually to become the owner of a farm home. A large number of our immigrants share with the native-born citizen this laudable ambition. Therefore there is a constant decrease of efficient farm labor by these upward movements.

At the same time, there is a receding column of farm owners who, through bad management, have become farm tenants, and who from farm tenants may become farm laborers. While the percentage of this class is small, there are nevertheless some who fail to make good, and, if they are tenants, farm for a living rather than as a business, and, if laborers, become watchers of the sun rather than efficient workers.

(a) STATEMENT OF THE GENERAL FARM LABOR PROBLEM.

The farm labor problem, however, is complicated by several special conditions, such as the fact that the need for labor is not continuous, the lack of conveniences of living for the laborer, long hours, the want of companionship, and in some places the apparently low wages. Because of these conditions, the necessary drift of workmen is from the open country to the town. On the part of the employer, the problem is complicated by the difficulty of securing labor, even at the relatively high prices now prevailing, that is competent to handle modern farm machinery and to care for live-stock and to handle the special work of the improved dairy. It is further complicated in all parts of the country by the competition of railroads, mines and factories, which, by reason of shorter hours, apparently higher pay, and the opportunities for social diversion and often of dissipation, attract the native farm hand to the towns and cities.

The difficulty of securing good labor is so great in many parts of the country that farmers are driven to dispose of their farms, leaving their land to be worked on shares by more or less irresponsible tenants, or selling them outright, often to foreigners. All absentee and proxy farming (which seems to be increasing) creates serious social problems in the regions thus affected. There is not sufficient good labor available in the country to enable us to farm our lands under present systems of agriculture and to develop our institutions effectively. Our native labor supply could be much increased by such hygienic measures as would lessen the unnecessary death-rate among country children and insure better health to workmen.

So long as the labor supply is not equal to the demand, the country cannot compete with the town in securing labor. The country must meet the essential conditions offered by the town; or change the kind of farming.

The most marked reaction to the labor difficulty is the change in modes of farm management, whereby farming is slowly adapting itself to the situation. In some cases this change is in the nature of more intensive and business-like methods whereby the farmer becomes able to secure a better class of labor and to employ it more continuously. More frequently, however, the change is in the nature of a simplification of the business and a less full and active farm life. In the sod regions of the Northeast the tendency is toward a simple or even a primitive nature-farming, with the maximum of grazing and meadow and the minimum of hand labor. In many states the more difficult lands are being given up and machinery-farming is extending. This results in an unequal development of the country as a whole, with a marked shift in the

social equilibrium. The only real solution of the
present labor problem must lie in improved
methods of farming. These improvements will
be forced by the inevitable depletion of soil
fertility under any and all one-crop systems in
every part of the country, and realized by the
adoption on the part of intelligent, progressive
farmers of a rotation of crops and a system of
husbandry that will enable them to employ their
labor by the year and thereby secure a higher
type of workman by providing him a home with
all its appurtenances. The development of local
industries will also contribute to the solution of
the problem.

The excessive hours of labor on farms must be
shortened. This will come through the working
out of the better farm scheme just mentioned, and
substituting planning for some of the muscular
work. Already in certain regions of well-sys-
tematized diversified farming the average hours
of labor are less than ten.

There is a growing tendency to rely on foreigners for the farm labor supply, although the
sentiment is very strong in some regions against
immigration. It is the general testimony that

the native American labor is less efficient and less reliable than much of the foreign labor. This is due to the fact that the American is less pressed by the dire necessity to labor and to save, and because the better class of laborers is constantly passing on to land-ownership on its own account. Because of their great industry and thrift, certain foreigners are gradually taking possession of the land in some regions, and it seems to be only a question of time until they will drive out the native stock in those regions.

The most difficult rural labor problem is that of securing household help on the average farm. The larger the farm, the more serious the problem becomes. The necessity of giving a suitable education to her children deprives the farm woman largely of home help; while the lure of the city with its social diversions, more regular hours of labor and its supposed higher respectability, deprives her of help bred and born in the country. Under these circumstances, she is compelled to provide the food that requires the least labor. This simple fact explains much of the lack of variety, in the midst of the greatest possible abundance, so often complained of on the farmer's table. The development of the creamery system over large sections of the country has relieved the farmer's wife of a heavy burden. This gives the hint for further improvement. The community laundering and other work could be done in an establishment connected with the creamery. Labor-saving appliances in the future will greatly lighten the burdens of those who are willing to use them. With the teaching of home subjects in the schools, household labor will again become respectable as well as easier and more interesting.

There is widespread conviction that the farmer must give greater attention to providing good quarters to laborers and to protect them from discouragement and from the saloon. The shortage of labor seems to be the least marked where the laborer is best cared for. It is certain that farming itself must be so modified and organized as to meet the labor problem at least half way. While all farmers feel the shortage of help, the Commission has found that the best farmers usually complain least about the labor difficulty.

7

(b) THE QUESTION OF INTEMPERANCE.

The liquor question has been emphasized to the Commission in all parts of the country as complicating the labor question. It seems to be regarded as a burning country life problem. Intemperance is largely the result of the barrenness of farm life, particularly of the lot of the hired man. The Commission has made no inquiry into intemperance as such, but it is impressed, from the testimony that has accumulated, that drunkenness is often a very serious menace to country life, and that the saloon is an institution that must be banished from at least all country districts and rural towns if our agricultural interests are to develop to the extent to which they are capable. The evil is specially damning in the South because it seriously complicates the race problem. Certain states have recently adopted prohibitory regulations, but liquor is shipped into dry territory from adjoining regions and the evil is thereby often increased. Dry territories must rouse themselves to self-preservation in the face of this grave danger, and legislation must be enacted that will protect them. When a state goes dry, it should be allowed to keep dry.

There is most urgent need for a quickened public sentiment on this whole question of intoxication in rural communities in order to relieve country life of one of its most threatening handicaps. At the same time it is incumbent on every person to exert his best effort to provide the open country with such intellectual and social interests as will lessen the appeal and attractiveness of the saloon.

(c) DEVOLOPING THE LOCAL ATTACHMENTS OF THE FARM LABORER.

The best labor, other things being equal, is resident labor. Such reorganization of agriculture must take place as will tend more and more to employ the man the year round and to tie him to the land. The employer bears a distinct responsibility to the laborer, and also to society, to house him well and to help him to contribute his part to the community welfare.

Eventually, some kind of school or training facilities must be provided for the farm laborer, to cause him to develop skill and to interest him intellectually in his work.

Some kind of simple saving institution should also be developed in order to encourage thrift on the part of the laborer. It would be well, also, to study systems of life insurance in reference to farm workmen. The establishment of postal savings banks should contribute towards greater stability of farm labor.

The development of various kinds of coöperative buying and selling associations might be expected to train workmen in habits of thrift, if the men were encouraged to join them.

5. Health in the Open Country.

Theoretically the farm should be the most healthful place in which to live, and there are numberless farm houses, especially of the farm-owner class, that possess most excellent modern sanitary conveniences. Still it is a fact that there are also numberless other farm houses, especially of the tenant class, and even numerous rural school-houses, that do not have the rudiments of sanitary arrangement. Health conditions in many parts of the open country, therefore, are in urgent need of betterment. There are many questions of nation-wide importance, such as soil, milk and water pollution; too much visiting in case of contagious diseases; patent medicines, advertising quacks and intemperance; feeding of offal to animals at local slaughterhouses and general unsanitary conditions of those houses not under federal or other rigid sanitary control; in some regions unwholesome and poorly prepared and monotonous diet; lack of recreation; too long hours of work.

Added to these and other conditions, are important regional questions, such as the extensive spread of the hook-worm disease in the Gulf-Atlantic states; the prevalence of typhoid fever and malaria; and other difficulties due to neglect in the localities.

In general, the rural population is less safeguarded by boards of health than is the urban population. The physicians are farther apart and are called in later in case of sickness, and in some districts medical attendance is relatively more expensive. The necessity for disease prevention is therefore self-evident, and it becomes even more emphatic when we recall that infection may be spread from farms to cities in the streams and also in the milk, meat, and other farm products. Quite aside from the humanitarian point of view, the aggregate annual loss to the nation from unsanitary conditions on the farms must, when expressed in money values, reach an enormous sum, and a betterment of these conditions is a nation-wide obligation.

There is great need for the teaching of the simplest and commonest laws of hygiene and sanitation in all the schools. The people need knowledge, and no traditions should prevent them from having it. How and what to eat, the nature of disease, the importance of fresh air, the necessity of physical training even on the farm, the ineffectiveness or even the danger of nostrums, the physical evils of intemperance, all should be known in some useful degree to every boy and girl on leaving school.

Some of the most helpful work in improving rural sanitary conditions and in relieving suffering, is now proceeding from women's organizations. This work should be encouraged in every way. We especially commend the suggestion that such organizations, and other interests, provide visiting nurses for rural communities, when they are needed.

We find urgent need for better supervision of public health in rural communities on the part of states and localities. The control is now likely to be exercised only when some alarming condition prevails. We think that the federal government should be given the right to send its health officers into the various states on request of these states, at any time, for the purpose of investigating and controlling public health; it does not now have this right except at quarantine stations, although it may attend to diseases of domestic animals. It should also engage in publicity work on this subject.

6. WOMAN'S WORK ON THE FARM.

Realizing that the success of country life depends in very large degree on the woman's part, the Commission has made special effort to ascertain the condition of women on the farm. Often this condition is all that can be desired, with home duties so organized that the labor is not excessive, with kindly coöperation on the part of husbands and sons, and with household machines and conveniences well provided. Very many farm homes in all parts of the country are provided with books and periodicals, musical instruments, and all the necessary amenities. There are good gardens and attractive premises, and a sympathetic love of nature and of farm life on the part of the entire family.

On the other hand, the reverse of these conditions often obtains, sometimes because of pioneer conditions and more frequently because of lack of prosperity and of ideals. Conveniences for outdoor work are likely to have precedence over those for household work.

The routine work of women on the farm is to prepare three meals a day. This regularity of duty recurs regardless of season, weather, planting, harvesting, social demands, or any other factor. The only differences in different seasons are those of degree rather than of kind. It follows, therefore, that whatever general hardships, such as poverty, isolation, lack of labor-saving devices, may exist on any given farm, the burden of these hardships falls more heavily on the farmer's wife than on the farmer himself. In general her life is more monotonous and the more isolated, no matter what the wealth or the poverty of the family may be.

The relief to farm women must come through a general elevation of country living. The women must have more helps. In particular, these matters may be mentioned: development of a coöperative spirit in the home; simplification of the diet in many cases; the building of convenient and sanitary houses; providing running water in the house, and also more mechanical helps; good and convenient gardens; a less exclusive ideal of money-getting on the part of the farmer; providing better means of communication, as telephones, roads, and reading-circles; and developing of women's organizations. These and other agencies should relieve the woman of many of her manual burdens on the one hand, and interest her in outside activities on the other. The farm woman should have sufficient free time and strength so that she may serve the community by participating in its vital affairs.

We have found good women's organizations in some country districts; but as a rule such organizations are few or even none, or, where they exist, they merely radiate from towns. Some of the stronger central organizations are now pushing the country phase of their work with vigor.

Mothers' clubs, reading-clubs, church societies, home economics organizations, farmers' institutes, and other associations can accomplish much for farm women. Some of the regular farmers' organizations are now giving much attention to domestic subjects, and women participate freely in the meetings. There is much need among country women themselves of a stronger organizing sense for real coöperative betterment. It is important, also, that all rural organizations that are attended chiefly by men, should discuss the home-making subjects, for the whole difficulty often lies with the attitude of the men.

There is the most imperative need that domestic, household and health questions be taught in all schools. The home may well be made the center of rural school teaching. The school is capable of changing the whole attitude of the home life and the part that women should play in the development of the best country living.

III

THE GENERAL CORRECTIVE FORCES THAT SHOULD BE SET IN MOTION

The ultimate need of the open country is the development of community effort and of social resources. Here and there the Commission has found a rural neighborhood in which the farmers and their wives come together frequently and effectively for social intercourse, but these instances seem to be infrequent exceptions. There is a general lack of wholesome societies that are organized on a social basis. In the region in which the Grange is strong, this need is best supplied.

There is need of the greatest diversity in country life affairs, but there is equal need of a social cohesion operating among all these affairs and tying them all together. This life must be developed, as we have said, directly from native or resident forces. It is neither necessary nor desirable that an exclusive hamlet system be brought about in order to secure these ends. The problem before the Commission is to suggest means whereby this development may be directed and hastened directly from the land.

The social disorder is usually unrecognized. If only the farms are financially profitable, the rural condition is commonly pronounced good. Country life must be made thoroughly attractive and satisfying as well as remunerative, and able to hold the center of interest throughout one's lifetime. With most persons this can come only with the development of a strong community sense or feeling. The first condition of a good country life, of course, is good and profitable farming. The farmer must be enabled to live comfortably. Much attention has been given to better farming, and the progress of a generation has been marked. Small manufacture and better handicrafts need now to receive attention, for the open country needs new industries and new interests. The schools must help to bring these things about.

The economic and industrial questions are, of course, of prime importance, and we have dealt with them; but they must all be studied in their relations to the kind of life that should ultimately be established in rural communities. The Commission will fail of its purpose if it confines itself merely to providing remedies or correctives for the present and apparent troubles of the farmer, however urgent and important these troubles may be. All these matters must be conceived of as incidents or parts in a large constructive program. We must begin a campaign for rural progress.

To this end, local government must be developed to its highest point of efficiency, and all agencies that are capable of furthering a better country life must be federated. It will be necessary to set the resident forces in motion by means of outside agencies, or at least to direct them, if we are to secure the best results. It is specially necessary to develop the coöperative spirit, whereby all people participate and all become partakers.

The cohesion that is so marked among the different classes of farm folk in older countries cannot be reasonably expected at this period in American development. Nor is it desirable that a stratified society should be developed in this country. We have here no remnants of a feudal system, fortunately no system of entail, and no clearly drawn distinction between agricultural and other classes. We are as yet a new country with undeveloped resources, many far-away pastures, which, as is well known, are always green and inviting. Our farmers have been moving and numbers of them have not yet become so well settled as to speak habitually of their farm as "home." We have farmers from every European nation and with every phase of religious belief often grouped in large communities, naturally drawn together by a common language and a common faith, and yielding but slowly to the dominating and controlling forces of American farm life. Even where there was once social organization, as in the New England town (or township), the competition of the newly settled West and the wonderful development of urban civilization have disintegrated it. The middle-aged farmer of the central states sells the old homestead without much hesitation or regret and moves westward to find a greater acreage for his sons and daughters. The farmer of the

middle west sells the old home and moves to the
mountain states, to the Pacific Coast, to the
South, to Mexico, or to Canada.

Even when permanently settled, the farmer
does not easily combine with others for financial
or social betterment. The training of generations has made him a strong individualist, and he
has been obliged to rely mainly on himself. Self-
reliance being the essence of his nature, he does
not at once feel the need of coöperation for business purposes or of close association for social
objects. In the main, he has been prosperous,
and has not felt the need of coöperation. If he
is a strong man, he prefers to depend on his own
ability. If he is ambitious for social recognition,
he usually prefers the society of the town to that
of the country. If he wishes to educate his children, he avails himself of the schools of the city.
He does not as a rule dream of a rural organization that can supply as completely as the city
the four great requirements of man—health,
education, occupation, society. While his brother
in the city is striving by moving out of the business section into the suburbs to get as much as
possible of the country in the city, he does not

dream that it is possible to have most that is best of the city in the country.

The time has come when we must give as much attention to the constructive development of the open country as we have given to other affairs. This is necessary not only in the interest of the open country itself, but for the safety and progress of the nation.

It is impossible, of course, to suggest remedies for all the shortcomings of country life. The mere statement of the conditions, as we find them, ought of itself to challenge attention to the needs. We hope that this report of the Commission will accelerate all the movements that are now in operation for the betterment of country life. Many of these movements are beyond the reach of legislation. The most important thing for the Commission to do is to apprehend the problem and to state the conditions.

The philosophy of the situation requires that the disadvantages and handicaps that are not a natural part of the farmer's business shall be removed, and that such forces shall be encouraged and set in motion as will stimulate and direct local initiative and leadership.

The situation calls for concerted action. It must be aroused and energized. The remedies are of many kinds and they must come slowly. We need a redirection of thought to bring about a new atmosphere, and a new social and intellectual contact with life. This means that the habits of the people must change. The change will come gradually, of course, as a result of new leadership; and the situation must develop its own leaders.

Care must be taken in all the reconstructive work to see that local initiative is relied on to the fullest extent, and that federal and even state agencies do not perform what might be done by the people in the communities. The centralized agencies should be stimulative and directive, rather than mandatory and formal. Every effort must be made to develop native resources not only of material things but also of people.

It is necessary to be careful, also, not to copy too closely the reconstructive methods that have been so successful in Europe. Our conditions and problems differ widely from theirs. We have no historical social peasantry, a much less centralized form of government, unlike systems

8

of land occupancy, wholly different farming schemes and different economic and social systems. Our country necessities are peculiarly American.

The correctives for the social sterility of the open country are already in existence or under way, but these agencies all need to be strengthened and especially to be coördinated and federated; and the problem needs to be recognized by all the people. The regular agricultural departments and institutions are aiding in making farming profitable and attractive, and they are also giving attention to the social and community questions. There is a widespread awakening, as a result of this work. This awakening is greatly aided by the rural free delivery of mails, telephones, the gradual improvement of highways, farmers' institutes, coöperative creameries and similar organizations, and other agencies.

The good institutions of cities may often be applied or extended to the open country. It appears that the social evils are in many cases no greater in cities in proportion to the number of people than in country districts; and the very concentration of numbers draws attention to the evils in cities and leads to earlier application of remedies. Recently much attention has been directed, for example, to the subject of juvenile crime, and the probation system in place of jail sentences for young offenders is being put into operation in many places. Petty crime and immorality are certainly not lacking in rural districts, and it would seem that there is a place for the extension of the probation system to towns and villages.

Aside from the regular churches, schools and agricultural societies, there are special organizations that are now extending their work to the open country, and others that could readily be adapted to country work. One of the most promising of these newer agencies is the rural library that is interested in its community. The libraries are increasing, and they are developing a greater sense of responsibility to the community, not only stimulating the reading habit and directing it, but becoming social centers for the neighborhood. A library, if provided with suitable rooms, can afford a convenient meeting-place for many kinds of activities and thereby serve as a coördinating influence. Study clubs and travelling libraries may become parts of it. This may mean that the library will need itself to be redirected, so that it will become an active rather than a passive agency; it must be much more than a collection of books.

Another new agency is the county work of the Young Men's Christian Association which, by placing in each county a field secretary, is seeking to promote the solidarity and effectiveness of rural social life, and to extend the larger influence of the country church. The Commission has met the representatives of this county work at the hearings, and is impressed with the purpose of the movement to act as a coördinating agency in rural life.

The organizations in cities and towns that are now beginning to agitate the development of better play, recreation and entertainment offer a suggestion for country districts. It is important that recreation be made a feature of country life, but we consider it to be important that this recreation, games and entertainment, be developed as far as possible from native sources rather than to be transplanted as a kind of theatricals from exotic sources.

Other organizations that are helping the country social life, or that might be made to help it, are women's clubs, musical clubs, reading-clubs, athletic and playground associations, historical and literary societies, local business men's organizations and chambers of commerce, all genuinely coöperative business societies, civic and village improvement societies, local political organizations, granges and other fraternal organizations, and all groups that associate with the church and school.

There is every indication, therefore, that the social life of the open country is in process of improvement, although the progress at the present moment has not been great. The leaders need to be encouraged by an awakened public sentiment and all the forces should be so related to each other as to increase their total effectiveness while not interfering with the autonomy of any of them.

The proper correctives of the underlying structural deficiencies of the open country are knowledge, education, coöperative organizations, and personal leadership. These we may now discuss in more detail.

7. NEED OF AGRICULTURAL OR COUNTRY LIFE
SURVEYS.

The time has now come when we should know
in detail what our agricultural resources are. We
have long been engaged in making geological
surveys, largely with a view to locating our miner-
eral wealth. The country has been explored and
mapped. The main native resources have been
located in a general way. We must now know
what are the capabilities of every agricultural
locality, for agriculture is the basis of our prosperity and farming is always a local business.
We cannot make the best and most permanent
progress in the developing of a good country life
until we have completed a very careful inventory
of the entire country.

This inventory or census should take into
account the detailed topography and soil conditions of the localities, the local climate, the
whole character of streams and forests, the agricultural products, the cropping systems now in
practice, the conditions of highways, markets,
facilities in the way of transportation and communication, the institutions and organizations,
the adaptability of the neighborhood to the es-

tablishment of handicrafts and local industries, the general economic and social status of the people and the character of the people themselves, natural attractions and disadvantages, historical data, and a collation of community experience. This would result in the collection of local fact, on which we could proceed to build a scientifically and economically sound country life.

Beginnings have been made in several states in the collection of these geographical facts, mostly in connection with the land-grant colleges. The United States Department of Agriculture is beginning by means of soil surveys, study of farm management and other investigations; and its demonstration work in the Southern states is in part of this character. These agencies are beginning the study of conditions in the localities themselves. It is a kind of extension work. All these agencies are doing good work; but we have not yet as a people come to an appreciation of the fact that we must take account of stock in detail as well as in the large. We are working mostly around the edges of the problem, and feeling of it. The larger part of the responsibility of this work must lie with the different states, for they should develop their internal resources. The whole work should be coördinated, however, by federal agencies acting with the states, and some of the larger relations will need to be studied directly by the federal government itself. We must come to a thoroughly nationalized movement to understand what property we have and what uses may best be made of it. This in time will call for large appropriations by state and nation.

In estimating our natural resources, we must not forget the value of scenery. This is a distinct asset, and it will be more recognized as time goes on. It will be impossible to develop a satisfactory country life without conserving all the beauty of landscape, and developing the people to the point of appreciating it. In parts of the East, a regular system of parking the open country of the entire state is already begun, constructing the roads, preserving the natural features and developing the latent beauty in such a way that the whole country becomes part of one continuing landscape treatment. This in no way interferes with the agricultural utilization of the land, but rather increases it. The scenery is in fact, capitalized, so that it adds to the property values and contributes to local patriotism and to the thrift of the commonwealth.

8. NEED OF A REDIRECTED EDUCATION.

The subject of paramount importance in our correspondence and in the hearings is education. In every part of the United States there seems to be one mind, on the part of those capable of judging, on the necessity of redirecting the rural schools. There is no such unanimity on any other subject. It is remarkable with what similarity of phrase the subject has been discussed in all parts of the country before the Commission. Everywhere there is a demand that education have relation to living, that the schools should express the daily life, and that in the rural districts they should educate, by means of agriculture and country life subjects. It is recognized that all difficulties resolve themselves in the end into a question of education.

The schools are held to be largely responsible for ineffective farming, lack of ideals, and the drift to town. This is not because the rural schools, as a whole, are declining, but because they are in a state of arrested development and have not yet put themselves in consonance with all the recently changed conditions of life. The very forces that have built up the city and town school have caused the neglect of the country school. It is probable that the farming population will willingly support better schools as soon as it becomes convinced that the schools will really be changed in such a way as to teach persons how to live.

The country communities are in need of social centers,—places where persons may naturally meet, and where a real neighborhood interest exists. There is difference of opinion as to where this center should be, some persons thinking it should be in the town or village, others the library, others the church or school or grange hall. It is probable that more than one social center should develop in large and prosperous communities. Inasmuch as the school is supported by public funds and is therefore an institution connected with the government of the community, it should form a natural organic center. If the school develops such a center, it must concern itself directly with the interests of the people. It is difficult to make people understand what this really means, for school-teaching is burdened with tradition. The school must express the best coöperation of all social and economic forces that make for the welfare of the community. Merely to add new studies will not meet the need, although it may break the ground for new ideas. The school must be fundamentally redirected, until it becomes a new kind of institution. This will require that the teacher himself be a part of the community and not a migratory factor.

The feeling that agriculture must color the work of rural public schools is beginning to express itself in the interest in nature-study, in the introduction of classes in agriculture in high-schools and elsewhere, and in the establishment of separate or special schools to teach farm and home subjects. These agencies will help to bring about the complete reconstruction of which we have been speaking. It is specially important that we make the most of the existing public school system, for it is this very system that should serve the real needs of the people. The real needs of the people are not alone the arts by which they make a living, but the whole range of their customary activities. As the home is the center of our civilization, so the home subjects should be the center of every school.

The most necessary thing now to be done for public school education in terms of country life is to rouse all the people to the necessity of such education, to coördinate the forces that are beginning to operate, and to project the work beyond the schools for youth into continuation schools for adults. The schools must represent and express the community in which they stand, although, of course, they should not be confined to the community. They should teach health and sanitation, even if it is necessary to modify the customary teaching of physiology. The teaching should be visual, direct and applicable. Of course, the whole tendency of the schools will be ethical if they teach the vital subjects truthfully; but particular care should be taken that they stand for the morals of the pupils and of the communities.

We find a general demand for federal encouragement in educational propaganda, to be in some way coöperative with the states. The people realize that the incubus of ignorance and inertia is so heavy and so widespread as to constitute a national danger, and that it should be removed as rapidly as possible. It will be increasingly necessary for the national and state governments to coöperate to bring about the results that are needed in agricultural and other industrial education.

The consideration of the educational problem raises the greatest single question that has come before the Commission, and which the Commission has to place before the American people. Education has now come to have vastly more significance than the mere establishing and maintaining of schools. The education motive has been taken into all kinds of work with the people, directly in their homes and on their farms, and it reaches mature persons as well as youths. Beyond and behind all educational work there must be an aroused intelligent public sentiment; to make this sentiment is the most important work immediately before us. The whole country is alive with educational activity. While this activity may all be good, it nevertheless needs to be directed and correlated, and all the agencies should be more or less federated.

The arousing of the people must be accomplished in terms of their daily lives, or of their welfare. For the country people this means that it must be largely in terms of agriculture. Some of the colleges of agriculture are now doing this kind of work effectively, although on a pitiably small scale as compared with the needs. This is extension work, by which is meant all kinds of educational effort directly with the people, both old and young, at their homes and on their farms; it comprises all educational work that is conducted away from the institution and for those who cannot go to schools and colleges. The best extension work now proceeding in this country— if measured by the effort to reach the people in their homes and on their own ground—is that coming from some of the colleges of agriculture and the United States Department of Agriculture. Within the last five or ten years, the colleges of agriculture have been able to attack the problem of rural life in a new way. This extension work includes such efforts as local agricultural surveys, demonstrations on farms, nature-study and other work in schools, boys' and girls' clubs of many kinds, crop organizations, redirection of rural societies, reading-clubs, library extension, lectures, travelling-schools, farmers' institutes, inspections of herds, barns, crops, orchards and farms, publications of many kinds, and similar educational effort directly in the field.

To accomplish these ends, we suggest the establishment of a nation-wide extension work. The first or original work of the agricultural branches of the land-grant colleges was academic in the old sense; later there was added the great field of experiment and research; there now should be added the third coördinate branch, comprising extension work, without which no college of agriculture can adequately serve its state. It is to the extension department of these colleges, if properly conducted, that we must now look for the most effective rousing of the people on the land.

In order that all public educational work in the United States may be adequately studied and guided, we also recommend that the United States Bureau of Education be enlarged and supported in such a way that it will really represent the educational activities of the nation, becoming a clearing-house, and a collecting, distributing and investigating organization. It is now wholly inadequate to accomplish these ends. In a country in which education is said to be the national religion, this condition of our one expressly federal educational agency is pathetic. The good use already made of the small appropriations provided for the Bureau, shows clearly hat it can render a most important service ift sufficient funds are made available for its use.

9. NECESSITY OF WORKING TOGETHER.

It is of the greatest consequence that the people of the open country should learn to work together, not only for the purpose of forwarding their economic interests and of competing with other men who are organized, but also to develop themselves and to establish an effective community spirit. This effort should be a genuinely coöperative or common effort in which all the associated persons have a voice in the management of the organization and share proportionately in its benefits. Many of the so-called "coöperative" organizations are really not such, for they are likely to be controlled in the interest of a few persons rather than for all and with no thought of the good of the community at large. Some of the societies that are coöperative in name are really strong centralized corporations or stock companies that have no greater interest in the welfare of the patrons than other corporations have.

At present the coöperative spirit works itself out chiefly in business organizations, devoted to selling and buying. So far as possible, these business organizations should have more or less social uses; but even if the organizations cannot be so used, the growth of the coöperative spirit should of itself have great social value, and it should give the hint for other coöperating groups. There is great need of associations in which persons coöperate directly for social results. The primary coöperation is social and should arise in the home, between all members of the family.

The associations that have an educational purpose are very numerous, such as the common agricultural societies and clubs devoted to stock-raising, fruit-growing, grain-growing, poultry-keeping, floriculture, bee-culture, and the like,

9

mostly following the lines of occupation. These are scarcely truly coöperative, since they usually do not effect a real organization to accomplish a definite end, and they may meet only once or twice a year; they hold conventions, but usually do not maintain a continuous activity. These societies are the greatest benefit, however, and they have distinct social value. No doubt a great many of them could be so reorganized or developed as to operate continuously throughout the year and become truly coöperative in effort, thereby greatly increasing their influence and importance.

A few great farmers' organizations have included in their declarations of purposes the whole field of social, educational and economic work. Of such, of national scope, are Patrons of Husbandry and the Farmers' Union. These and similar large societies are effective in proportion as they maintain local branches that work toward specific ends in their communities.

While there are very many excellent agricultural coöperative organizations of many kinds, the farmers nearly everywhere complain that there is still a great dearth of association that really helps them in buying and selling and developing their communities. Naturally, the effective coöperative groups are in the most highly developed communities; the general farmer is yet insufficiently helped by the societies. The need is not so much for a greater number of societies as for a more complete organization within them and for a more continuous active work.

Farmers seem to be increasingly feeling the pressure of the organized interests that sell to them and buy from them. They complain of business understandings or agreements between all dealers from the wholesaler and jobber to the remote country merchants, that prevent farmers and their organizations from doing an independent business.

The greatest pressure on the farmer is felt in regions of undiversified one-crop farming. Under such conditions, he is subject to great risk of crop failure; his land is soon reduced in productiveness; he usually does not raise his home supplies, and is therefore dependent on the store for his living; and his crop, being a staple and produced in enormous quantities, is subject to world prices and to speculation, so that he has no personal market. In the exclusive cotton and wheat regions, the hardships of the farmer and the monotony of rural life are usually very marked. Similar conditions are likely to obtain in large-area stock-ranging, hay-raising, tobacco-growing and the like. In such regions, great discontent is likely to prevail and economic heresies to breed. The remedy is diversification in farming on the one hand, and organization on the other.

The Commission has found many organizations that seem to be satisfactorily handling the transporting, distributing and marketing of farm products. They are often incorporated stock companies in which the coöperators have the spur of money investment to hold them to their mutual obligations. In nearly all cases, the most successful organizations are in regions that are strongly dominated by similar products, as fruit, dairy, grain, or live-stock.

Two principles may be applied in these business societies: in one class, the organization is in the nature of a combination, and attempts to establish prices and perhaps to control the production;

in the other class, the organization seeks its results by studying and understanding the natural laws of trade and taking advantage of conditions and regulating such evils as may arise, in the same spirit as a merchant studies them, or as a good farmer understands the natural laws of fertility.

With some crops, notably cotton and the grains, it is advantageous to provide coöperative warehouses in which the grower may hold his products till prices rise; and also in which scientific systems of grading of the products may be introduced. In certain fruit regions, community packing-houses have proved to be of the greatest benefit. In the meantime the cotton or grain in the warehouse becomes, for business purposes, practically as good as cash (subject to charge for insurance) in the form of negotiable warehouse receipts. This form of handling products is now coming to be well understood, and, combined with good systems of farming, it is capable of producing most satisfactory results.

Organized effort must come as the voluntary expression of the people; but it is essential that every state should enact laws that will stimulate and facilitate the organization of such coöperative associations, care being taken that the working of the laws be not cumbersome. These laws should provide the association with every legal facility for the transaction of the business in which they are to engage. They are as important to the state as other organizations of capital, and should be fostered with as much care, and their members and patrons be adequately safeguarded. It is especially important that these organizations be granted all the powers and advantages given to corporations or other aggregations of capital, to the end that they may meet these corporations on equal legal ground when it is necessary to compete with them. Such laws should not only protect the coöperative societies, but should provide means that will allow the societies to regulate themselves, so that they may be safeguarded from becoming merely commercial organizations through the purchase or control of the stock by dealers in the products that they handle. It is not unlikely that federal laws may also be needed to encourage coöperation.

Organized associative effort may take on special forms. It is probable, for example, that coöperation to secure and to employ farm labor would be helpful. It may have for its object the securing of telephone service (which is already contributing much to country life and is capable of contributing much more), the extension of electric lines, the improvement of highways, and other forms of betterment. Particular temporary needs of the neighborhood may be met by combined effort, and this may be made the beginning of a broader permanent organization.

A method of coöperative credit would undoubtedly prove of great service. In other countries credit associations loan money to their members on easy terms and for long enough time to cover the making of a crop, demanding security not on the property of the borrower, but on the moral warranty of his character and industry. The American farmer has needed money less, perhaps, than land-workers in some other countries, but he could be greatly benefitted by a different system of credit, particularly where the lien system is still in operation. It would be the purpose of such systems, aside from providing loans on the best terms and with the utmost freedom consistent with safety, to keep as much as possible of the money in circulation in the open country where the values originate. The present banking systems tend to take the money out of the open country and to loan it in town or to town-centered interests. We suggest that the national bank examiners be instructed to determine, for a series of years, what proportion of the loanable funds of rural banks is loaned to the farmers in their localities, in order that data may be secured on this question. All unnecessary drain from the open country should be checked, in order that the country may be allowed and encouraged to develop itself.

It is essential that all rural organizations, both social and economic, should develop into something like a system, or at least that all the efforts be known and studied by central authorities. There should be, in other words, a voluntary union of associative effort, from the localities to the counties, states, and the nation. Manifestly, government in the United States cannot manage the work of voluntary rural organization. Personal initiative and a cultivated cooperative spirit are the very core of this kind of work; yet both state and national government, as suggested, might exert a powerful influence toward the complete organization of rural affairs.

Steps should be taken whereby the United States Department of Agriculture, the state departments of agriculture, the land-grant colleges and experiment stations, the United States Bureau of Education, the normal and ether schools, shall coöperate in a broad program for aiding country life in such a way that each institution may do its appropriate work at the same time that it aids all the others and contributes to the general effort to develop a new rural social life.

10. THE COUNTRY CHURCH.

This Commission has no desire to give advice to the institutions of religion nor to attempt to dictate their policies. Yet any consideration of the problem of rural life that leaves out of account the function and the possibilities of the church, and of related institutions, would be grossly inadequate. . This is not only because in the last analysis the country life problem is a moral problem, or that in the best development of the individual the great motives and results are religious and spiritual, but because from the pure sociological point of view the church is fundamentally a necessary institution in country life. In a peculiar way the church is intimately related to the agricultural industry. The work and the life of the farm are closely bound together, and the institutions of the country react on that life and on one another more intimately than they do in the city. This gives the rural church a position of peculiar difficulty and one of unequalled opportunity. The time has arrived when the church must take a larger leadership, both as an institution and through its pastors, in the social reorganization of rural life.

The great spiritual needs of the country community just at present are higher personal and community ideals. Rural people need to have an aspiration for the highest possible development of the community. There must be an ambition on the part of the people themselves constantly to progress in all of those things that make the community life wholesome, satisfying, educative and complete. There must be a desire to develop a permanent environment for the country boy and girl, of which they will become passionately fond. As a pure matter of education, the countryman must learn to love the country and to have an intellectual appreciation of it. More than this, the spiritual nature of the individual must be kept thoroughly alive. His personal ideals of conduct and ambition must be cultivated.

Of course the church has an indispensable function as a conservator of morals. But from the social point of view, it is to hold aloft the torch of personal and community idealism. It must be a leader in the attempt to idealize country life.

The country church doubtless faces special difficulties. As a rule it is a small field. The country people are conservative. Ordinarily the financial support is inadequate. Often there are too many churches in a given community. Sectarian ideas divide unduly and unfortunately. While there are many rural churches that are effective agents in the social evolution of their communities, it is true that as a whole the coun-

try church needs new direction and to assume
new responsibilities. Few of the churches in
the open country are provided with resident
pastors. They are supplied mostly from the
neighboring towns and by a representative of
some single denomination. Sometimes the pul-
pit is supplied by pastors of different denominations in turn. Without a resident minister the
church work is likely to be confined chiefly to
services once a week. In many regions there
is little personal visitation except in cases of
sickness, death, marriage, christening or other
special circumstance. The Sunday School is
sometimes continued only during the months
of settled weather. There are young people's
organizations to some extent, but they are often
inactive or irregular. The social activity of
the real country church is likely to be limited
to the short informal meetings before and after
services and to suppers that are held for the
purpose of raising funds. Most of the gatherings are designed for the church people themselves rather than for the community. The
range of social influence is therefore generally
restricted to the families particularly related

to the special church organization, and there is likely to be no sense of social responsibility for the entire community.

In the rural villages there are generally several or a number of churches of different denominations, one or more of which are likely to be weak. The salaries range from $400 to $1,000. Among Protestants there is considerable denominational competition and consequent jealousy or even conflict. United effort for coöperative activity is likely to be perfunctory rather than sympathetic and vital. The pastor is often overloaded with station work in neighboring communities.

It is not the purpose of the Commission to discuss the difficulties of the rural church at this time nor to present a solution for them, but, in the interests of rural betterment, it seems proper to indicate a few considerations that seem to be fundamental.

(1) In New England and in some other parts of the North, the tremendous drawback of denominational rivalry is fairly well recognized and active measures for church federation are well under way. This does not mean organic union. It means coöperation for the purpose of

trying to reach and influence every individual in the community. It means that " some church is to be responsible for every square mile." When a community is over-churched, it means giving up the superfluous church or churches. When a church is needed, it means a friendly agreement on the particular church to be placed there. This movement for federation is one of the most promising in the whole religious field, because it does not attempt to break down donominational influence or standards of thought. It puts emphasis, not on the church itself, but on the work to be done by the church for all men, churched and unchurched. It is possible that all parts of the country are not quite ready for federation, although a national church federation movement is under way. But it hardly seems necessary to urge that the spirit of coöperation among churches, the diminution of sectarian strife, the attempt to reach the entire community, must become the guiding principles everywhere if the rural church is long to retain its hold.

(1) The rural church must be more completely than now a social center. This means not so much a place for holding social gatherings,

although this is legitimate and desirable, but a place whence constantly emanates influences that go to build up the moral and spiritual tone of the whole community. The country church of the future is to be held responsible for the great ideals of community life as well as of personal character.

(2) There should be a large extension of the work of the Young Men's Christian Association into the rural communities. There is apparently no other way to grip the hearts and lives of the boys and young men of the average country neighborhood. This association must regard itself as an ally of the church, with a special function and a special field.

(3) We must have a complete conception of the country pastorate. The country pastor must be a community leader. He must know the rural problems. He must have sympathy with rural ideals and aspirations. He must love the country. He must know country life, the difficulties that the farmer has to face in his business, some of the great scientific revelations made in behalf of agriculture, the great industrial forces at work for the making or the unmaking of the farmer,

the fundamental social problems of the life of
the open country.

Consequently, the rural pastor must have
special training for his work. Ministerial colleges and theological seminaries should unite
with agricultural colleges in this preparation of
the country clergyman. There should be better
financial support for the clergyman; in many
country districts it is pitiably small. There is
little incentive for a man to stay in a country
parish, and yet this residence is just what must
come about. Perhaps it will require an appeal
to the heroic young men, but we must have more
men going into the country pastorates not as a
means of getting a foothold but as a permanent
work. The clergyman has an excellent chance for
leadership in the country. In some sections he is
still the dominating personality. But everywhere
he may become one of the great community
leaders. He is the key to the country church
problem.

11. Personal Ideals and Local Leadership.

Everything resolves itself at the end into a
question of personality. Society, or government,

cannot do much for country life unless there is voluntary response in the personal ideals of those who live in the country. Inquiries by the Commission, for example, find that one reason for the shift from the country to town is the lack of ideals in many country homes and even the desire of the countryman and his wife that the children do not remain on the farm. The obligation to keep as many youths on the farms as are needed there, rests on the home more than on the school or on society.

It is often said that better rural institutions and more attractive homes and yards will necessarily follow an increase in profitableness of farming; but as a matter of fact, high ideals may be quite independent of income, although they cannot be realized without sufficient income to provide good support. Many of the most thrifty farmers are the least concerned about the character of the home and school and church. One often finds the most attractive and useful farm homes in the difficult farming regions. On the other hand, some of the most prosperous agricultural regions possess most unattractive farm premises and school buildings. Many persons

10

who complain most loudly about their incomes
are the last to improve their home conditions
when their incomes are increased; they are more
likely to purchase additional land and thereby
further emphasize the barrenness of home life.
Land-hunger is naturally strongest in the most
prosperous regions.

When an entire region or industry is not
financially prosperous, it is impossible, of course,
to develop the best personal and community
ideals. In the cotton-growing states, for example,
the greatest social and mental development has
been apparent in the years of high prices for
cotton; and the same is true in exclusive wheat
regions, hay regions, and other large areas
devoted mainly to one industry.

While it is of course necessary that the farmer
receive good remuneration for his efforts, it is
nevertheless true that the money consideration
is frequently too exclusively emphasized in farm
homes. This consideration often obscures every
other interest, allowing little opportunity for the
development of the intellectual, social and moral
qualities. The open country abounds in men and
women of the finest ideals; yet it is necessary to

say that other ends in life than the making of more money and the getting of more goods are much needed in country districts; and that this, more than anything else, will correct the unsatisfying nature of rural life.

Teachers of agriculture have placed too much relative emphasis on the remuneration and production sides of country life.   Money-hunger is as strong in the open country as elsewhere, and as there are fewer opportunities and demands for the expenditure of this money for others and for society, there often develops a hoarding and a lack of public spirit that is disastrous to the general good.   So completely does the money-purpose often control the motive, that other purposes in farming remain dormant.   The complacent contentment in many rural neighborhoods is itself the very evidence of social incapacity or decay.

It must not be assumed that these deficiencies are to be charged as a fault against the farmer as a group.   They are rather to be looked on as evidence of an uncorrelated and unadjusted society.   Society is itself largely to blame.   The social structure has been unequally developed.

The townsman is likely to assume superiority and to develop the town in disregard of the real interests of the open country or even in opposition to them. The city exploits the country; the country does not exploit the city. The press still delights in archaic cartoons of the farmer. There is as much need of a new attitude on the part of the townsman as on the part of the farmer.

This leads us to say that the country ideals, while derived largely from the country itself, should not be exclusive; and the same applies to city and village ideals. There should be more frequent social intercourse on equal terms between the people of the country and those of the city or village. This community of interests is being accomplished to a degree at present, but there is hardly yet the knowledge and sympathy and actual social life that there should be between those who live on the land and those who do not. The business men's organizations of cities could well take the lead in some of this work. The country town in particular has similar interests with the open country about it; but beyond this, all people are bettered and broadened by association with those of far different environment.

We have now discussed some of the forces and agencies that will aid in bringing about a new rural society. The development of the best country life in the United States is seen, therefore, to be largely a question of guidance. The exercise of a wise advice, stimulus, and direction from some central national agency, extending over a series of years, could accomplish untold good, not only for the open country, but for all the people and for our institutions.

In the communities themselves, the same kind of guidance is needed, operating in good farming, in schools, churches, societies, and all useful public work. The great need everywhere is new and young leadership, and the Commission desires to make an appeal to all young men and women who love the open country to consider this field when determining their careers. We need young people of quality, energy, capacity, aspiration and conviction, who will live in the open country as permanent residents on farms, or as teachers, or in other useful fields, and who, while developing their own business or affairs to the greatest perfection, will still have unselfish interest in the welfare of their communities. The farming country is by no means devoid of leaders, and is not lost or incapable of helping itself, but it has been relatively overlooked by persons who are seeking great fields of usefulness. It will be well for us as a people if we recognize the opportunity for usefulness in the open country and consider that there is a call for service.

L. H. BAILEY.
HENRY WALLACE.
KENYON L. BUTTERFIELD.
WALTER H. PAGE.
GIFFORD PINCHOT.
C. S. BARRETT.
W. A. BEARD.

.